*The development of this volume was made possible
in part by a generous grant from the
Charles & M.R. Shapiro Foundation of Chicago, IL
in memory of Morris Shapiro*

D1591602

050 4ELLI

The Complete Jewish Songbook
for children!

201 Jewish songs for holidays,

ever   r fun!

or

U A H C

Preface to the Tenth Anniversary Reprint of
The Complete Jewish Songbook for Children: Manginot

Manginot – Songs – was originally conceived as the musical component of the UAHC Religious School curriculum *To See The World Through Jewish Eyes*, but through the past ten years it has taken on a life of its own. These 201 songs provide a musical picture of Jewish life in its many aspects, from cradle to the grave, encompassing holidays and festivals, celebrations and sadness.

Manginot went through many transformations before it reached its printed form, hundreds of songs and chants were examined and considered by a committee of cantors, rabbis and music professionals, to select those that would best reflect the goals of a supplementary school curriculum, while providing the students with an immersion into Jewish music.

This is music for the classroom: an aid in teaching Judaism which provides an experiential dimension to the learning process. Some of the songs are meant to be sung, others to be listened to; some of them engage the children in activities, others quiet them down. This book contains everything from pre-school songs to the holiest chant from Yom Kippur, *Kol Nidrei*. There are examples of biblical chant, *nuchaot* or traditional chants for the holidays, and fun tunes about Jewish symbols.

The songs are best taught as part of lessons on history, theology, Jewish identity, the Jewish people, Israel, holidays, Bible, Talmud and all other parts of Jewish life and learning. They may be taught by the classroom teacher, the music specialist or the cantor, but to be effective, they should be taught in context.

Recordings and books containing portions of the songs organized by age levels are available through Transcontinental Music Publications.

Special thanks are due to Cantors Vicki L. Axe, Samuel Dov Berman, Mark Elson, Jeffrey Klepper and Rabbis Lawrence P. Karol and Daniel H. Freelander for their help in the selection process; Rabbi Freelander and the Commission on Synagogue Music for their help with the project; to all the lyricists and composers who have given of their work and talent, and to Dr. Judith Tischler for her tough amd tireless proofreading, and for seeing this through the publication process.

Cantor Stephen Richards, Editor

THE COMPLETE JEWISH SONGBOOK FOR CHILDREN: MANGINOT
©2002 Transcontinental Music Publications/New Jewish Music Press
A Division of the Union of American Hebrew Congregations
633 Third Avenue - New York, NY 10017 - fax 212.650.4109
212.650.4101 - www.TranscontinentalMusic.com - tmp@uahc.org

Manufactured in the United States of America
Cover design by Joel N. Eglash
Cover art by Doreen Gay-Kassel
ISBN 8074-0820-4
10 9 8 7 6 5 4 3

The Complete Jewish Songbook for Children: Manginot
INDEX OF CATEGORIES

Songs from the Bible

Songs of Ethical Teaching
The Talmud and Tikun Olam

Hebrew Pronunciation Guide

VOWELS
a as in *father*
ai as in *aisle* (= long *i* as in *ice*)
e = short *e* as in *bed*
ei as in *eight* (= long *a* as in *ace*)
i as in *pizza* (= long *e* as in *be*)
o = long *o* as in *go*
u = long *u* as in *lunar*

CONSONANTS
ch as in German *Bach* or Scottish *loch* (not as in *cheese*)
g = hard *g* as in *get* (not soft *g* as in *gem*)
tz = as in *boats*
h after a vowel is silent

Yiddish Pronunciation Guide

VOWELS
a as in *father*
ai as in *aisle* (= long *i* as in *ice*)
e = short *e* as in *bed*
ei as in *eight* (= long *a* as in *ace*)
i as in *pizza* (= long *e* as in *be*)
o = long *o* as in *go*
u (between consonants) = *u* as in *put*
u (at end of word) = long *u* as in *lunar*

CONSONANTS
ch as in German *Bach* or Scottish *loch* (not as in *cheese*)
g = hard *g* as in *get* (not soft *g* as in *gem*)
tz = as in *boats*

1. HEIVEINU SHALOM ALEICHEM

Folk Song

May peace come to all of you.

הֲבֵאנוּ שָׁלוֹם עֲלֵיכֶם, עֲלֵיכֶם הֲבֵאנוּ שָׁלוֹם.

2. HINEI MAH TOV
Round

Psalms   **Folk Song**

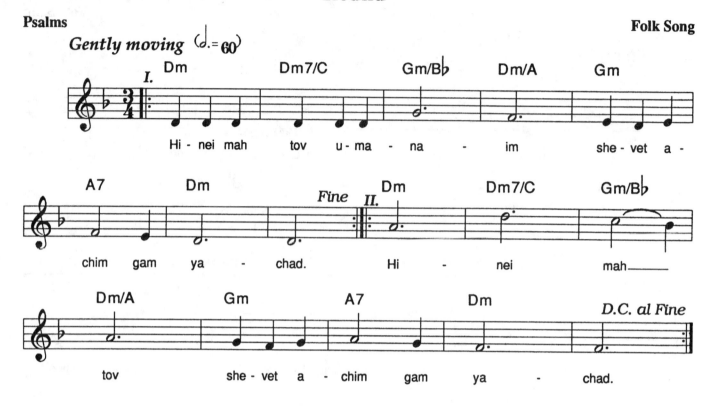

How good and pleasant it is for brothers and sisters to sit together.

הִנֵּה מַה טּוֹב וּמַה נָּעִים
שֶׁבֶת אַחִים גַּם יָחַד

3. GOOD MORNING, BOKER TOV

Words and Music by Judy Caplan Ginsburgh

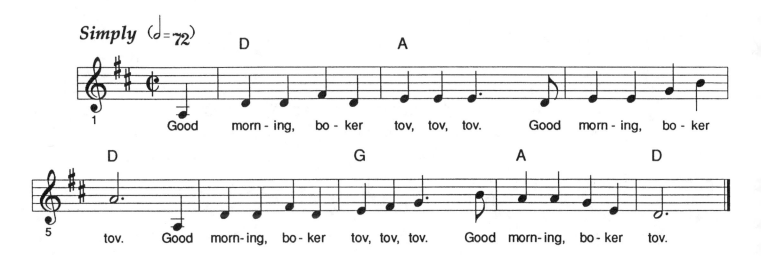

4. AM YISRAEL CHAI

Rabbi S. Carlebach

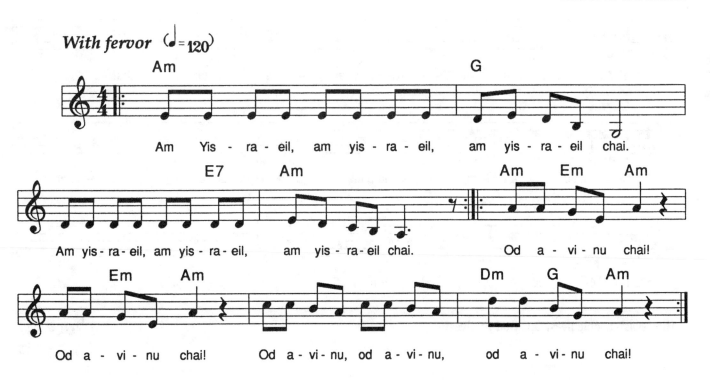

For Hebrew and translation
See number 5

5. AM YISRAEL CHAI

Rabbi Seymour Rockoff

The Jewish people lives! Our God yet lives!

עַם יִשְׂרָאֵל חַי
עוֹד אָבִינוּ חַי

6. NOW WE SAY SHALOM

Anonymous

Arranged by Stephen Richards

7. TZENAH, TZENAH
Round

Issachar Miron
J. Grossman (Part III)

Come out, O daughters and greet the soldiers.

צֶאנָה הַבָּנוֹת וּרְאֶינָה
חַיָלִים בַּמוֹשָׁבָה
אַל־נָא תִּתְחַבֵּאנָה
מִבֶּן־חַיִל אִישׁ צָבָא

8. AI DIDI DAI
Song Without Words

Chassidic Nigun

Arranged by Stephen Richards

9. TUMBALALAIKA

Folk Song

YIDDISH LYRICS

1. Shteyt a bocher un er tracht
Tracht un tracht a gantze nacht:
Vemen tsu nemen un nit farshemen?
Vemen tsu nemen un nit farshemen?

Refrain:

Tumbala, tumbala, tumbalalaika,
Tumbala, tumbala, tumbalalaika,
Tumbalalaika, shpiel balalaika,
Tumbalalaika, freilich sohl zein.

2. Meydl, meydl, ch'vel bay dir fregn:
Vos kon vaksn, vaksn on regn?
Vos kon brenen un nit oyfthrn?
Vos kon benken, veynen on trern?

3. Narisher bocher, vos darfstu fregn?
A shteyn kon vaksn, vaksn on regn.
Libe kon brenen, un nit oyfthern.
A harts kon benken, veynen on trern.

ENGLISH LYRICS

Once a lad was thinking all night,
How to find the girl that is right.
Whose heart to take and whose not to
   break?
Whose heart to take and whose not to
   break?

Refrain:

Tumbala, tumbala, tumbalalaika,
Tumbala, tumbala, tumbalalaika,
Tumbalalaika, shpiel balalaika,
Tumbalalaika, freilich sohl zein.

2. Maiden, maiden, tell me true,
What can grow, grow without dew?
What can burn for years and years?
What can cry and shed no tears?

3. Silly lad, here's the answer true:
A stone can grow, grow without dew.
Love can burn for years and years,
A heart can cry and shed no tears.

10. HAVAH NAGILAH

Chassidic Song
*Discovered and Adapted by Avraham Zvi Idelsohn
and Moshe Nathanson*

Come let us be glad and rejoice. Arise, brothers and sisters with a joyful heart.

הָבָה נָגִילָה וְנִשְׂמְחָה
עוּרוּ אַחִים בְּלֵב שָׂמֵחַ

11. LOS BILBILICOS

Ladino Folk Song

The nightingales sing with sighs of love.
My soul and my future are in your power.

The rose blooms today in the month of May.
My soul darkens like an eclipse of the moon.

12. ROJINKES MIT MANDLEN
Raisins and Almonds

Words and Music by Abraham Goldfaden

אין דעם בֵּית הַמִּקְדָּש אין אֵוינקל חֶדֶר
זיצְט די אַלְמָנָה בַּת צִיוֹן אַלֵיין
אִיהר בֶּן יָחִיד-ל אִידֶעלֶע וויגְט זִי כְּסֵדֶר
אוּן זִינְגְט אִיהם צום שְׁלָאפֿן אַ
לִידֶעלֶע שֵיין.
אוּנְטֶער אִידֶעלֶעס וויגֶעלֶע
שְׁטֵייט אַ קְלָאר ווֵיַיס צִיגֶעלֶע.
דָאס צִיגֶעלֶע אִיז גֶעפֿאָרן הַאַנְדְלֶען
דָאס ווֶעט זַיַין דַיַין בַּארוּף.
רָאזְשִׁינְקֶעס מִיט מַאַנְדְלֶען.
שְׁלָאף זֶשֶׁע אִידֶעלֶע שְׁלָאף!

In the Holy Temple, all alone in a corner
Sits the old widow, the Daughter of Zion.
And she rocks her young son, lying there in the cradle,
And sings him to sleep with this sweet lullaby.
'Neath the cradle of my young son stands a goat,
Yes, a pure white one.
The little goat has been fatted to wander,
That will be your fate, too.
Raisins sweet and almonds,
Sleep then, my little Jew
Sleep then, my little Jew

13. WORLD OF OUR FATHERS

Words and Music by Robert Solomon

Verse 1
Came to America in nineteen hundred four.
I was fleeing persecution and the army of the Tsar.
Reached Ellis Island, alone and half insane,
And I left there with a different name.

If it wasn't for my people, I don't know what I'd do,
And I thank the Lord above me that I was born a Jew.
They sheltered me and fed me 'til I got on my feet,
Then my mother's words came back to me:

Just don't forget where you came from, my son,
And the world of your father's, you'll soon leave behind.
Just keep the faith of your people wherever you go,
There a friend you will find.

Verse 2
Just another greenhorn looking for a job,
I prevailed upon a *landsman* to finally take me on.
Worked as a peddler ten hours every day;
In the evening I brought home my pay.

I scrimped and I saved 'til I put enough aside;
Then I sent it to my father, his passage for to buy.
Money for the steerage and money for the bribes.
It was four years since my mother died.

I won't forget where I came from, my Mother,
Each day in the synagogue I pray for you.
I've built a life for us here in America.
How proud you would be if you knew.

Verse 3
We worked to bring my sisters and my baby brother, too,
Then we moved to New England near some people that we knew.
I made a bit of money in Boston's old North End
Which we gradually learned how to spend.

A bunch of little citizens I brought into this world,
But most of them were no-goods who squandered while I toiled.
Sophisticate A0ericans they very soon became;
Of their father they would grow ashamed.

Just don't forget where you come from, my children.
The world of our fathers is what made us strong.
Don't sell your soul for the thrills of America;
What price must you pay to belong?

Verse 4
Been so many years, my grandchildren are grown,
And the one who is a doctor even keeps me in his home.
He says to me, "*Mein Zeide*, when the children learn to speak,
A *bissele Yiddish* you shall teach them."

There were times, so many times, when I feared that all was lost.
We had come so far, so fast, that I wondered what the cost.
But now I see my father's world begin to rise
In my great-grandchildren's eyes.

14. COLOR SONG

Adapted by Doris Sugar

after "Skip To My Lou"

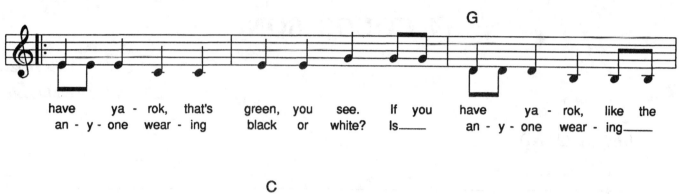

have ya - rok, that's green, you see. If you have ya - rok, like the
an - y - one wear - ing black or white? Is____ an - y - one wear - ing____

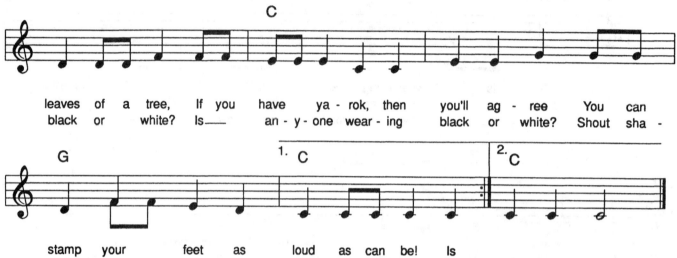

leaves of a tree, If you have ya - rok, then you'll ag - ree You can
black or white? Is____ an - y - one wear - ing black or white? Shout sha -

stamp your feet as loud as can be! Is
chor and la - van with_____ all your might!

15. AF, PEH, OZEN
Parts of the Body Song

Words and Music by Jeffrey Klepper

* Have children point
to the part of their body
as they sing its name.

Nose, Mouth, Ear, Leg, Hand and Head

אַף פֶּה אוֹזֶן עַיִן
רֶגֶל יָד וְרֹאשׁ

16. S'LICHAH, TODAH, B'VAKASHAH

English Verse by Shira Pasternak **Words and Music by Ella Shurin**

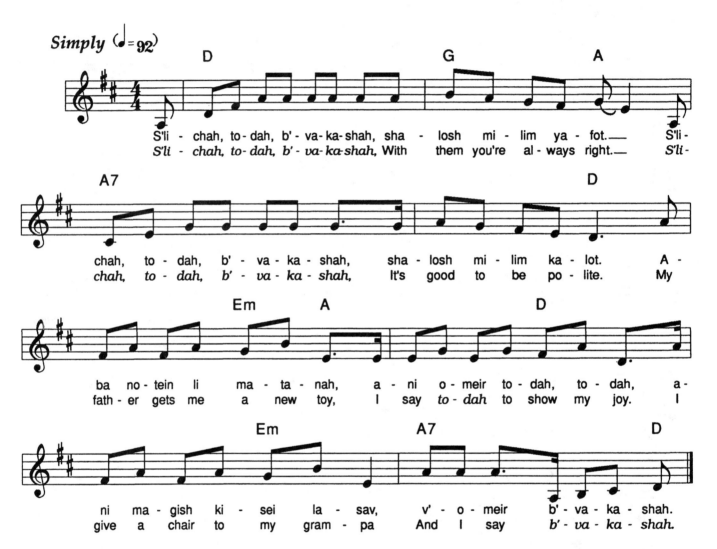

Excuse me, thank you, please,
Three pleasant words
Excuse me, thank you, please
Three easy words
Father gives me a gift
And I say thank you
I offer a chair to my father
And I say "Please"

סְלִיחָה תּוֹדָה בְּבַקָשָׁה
שָׁלֹשׁ מִלִּים יָפוֹת
אַבָּא נוֹתֵן לִי מַתָּנָה
אֲנִי אוֹמֵר תּוֹדָה
אֲנִי מַגִּישׁ כִּסֵּא לַסָב וְאוֹמֵר
בְּבַקָשָׁה

17. EEMA - ABA

Words and Music by Steven Carr Reuben

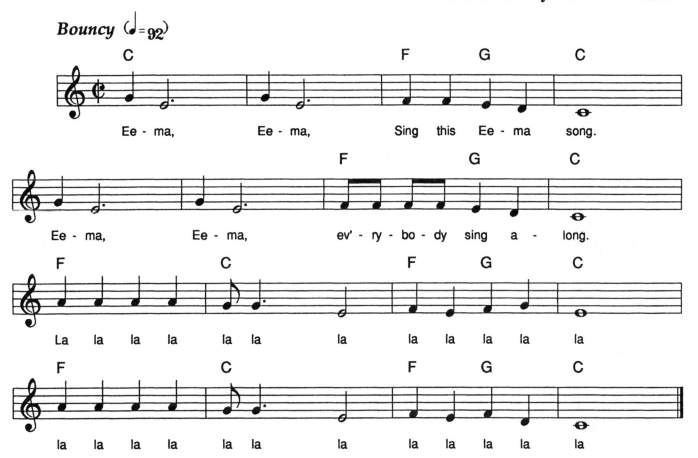

Eema, Eema, sing this Eema song.
Eema, Eema, everybody sing along.
La la la la la la la, la la la la la

Aba, Aba, sing this Aba song.
Aba, Aba, everybody sing along.
La la la la la la la, la la la la la

Eema, Eema, hee ba-mish-pa-cha.
Eema, Eema, tein la n'-shi-kah.
La la la la la la la, la la la la la

Aba, Aba, hu ba-mish-pa-cha.
Aba, Aba, tein lo n'-shi-kah.
La la la la la la la, la la la la la

Shabbat, Shabbat, sing this Shabbat song.
Shabbat, Shabbat, everybody sing along.
La la la la la la la, la la la la la

Neirot, neirot, see the candles shine.
Neirot, neirot, now it's Shabbat time.
La la la la la la la, la la la la la

Kiddush, kiddush, we all bless the wine.
Kiddush, kiddush, blessing yours and mine.
La la la la la la la, la la la la la

Challah, challah, tear the bread in two.
Challah, challah, share with me and you.
La la la la la la la, la la la la la

18. I'M GROWING

Words and Music by Jeffrey Klepper

I'm grow-in', grow-in', grow-in' grow-in' old-er ev'-ry day. I'm grow-in', grow-in', grow-in', grow-in' up in diff-'rent ways. Grow-ing up like an-y boy or girl,—— a mem-ber of—— this great big world, But I'm al-so grow-ing Jew-ish-ly,—— and that—— means a lot to me.——

19. MISHPACHA SONG

Words and Music by Daniel Syme

Chorus
I want you to meet my family.
In Hebrew, we call it "Mish-pa-cha."
We all live in a "Bayit,"
Me, my ma and pa.

Verse 1.
There's my father, that's "Aba," say "Aba."
There's my mother, that's "Eema," say "Eema."
And these are the members of my family.
My family, that's my family.

Verse 2.
There's my brother, that's "Ach," say "Ach."
There's my sister, that's "Achot," say "Achot."
There's my father, that's "Aba," say "Aba."
There's my mother, that's "Eema," say "Eema."
And these are the members of my family.
My family, that's my family.

Verse 3.
There's my grandpa, that's "Saba," say "Saba."
There's my grandma, that's "Savta," say "Savta."
There's my brother, that's "Ach," say "Ach."
There's my sister, that's "Achot," say "Achot."
There's my father, that's "Aba," say "Aba."
There's my mother, that's "Eema," say "Eema."
And these are the members of my family.
My family, that's my family.

20. WE SAY "SHEHECHEYANU, THANK YOU, GOD"

Words and Music by Jeffrey Klepper

21. WITH MY FAMILY

Words and Music by Jeffrey Klepper

Dm7 **G** **F** **Em** **Dm7** **Gsus4**

ve - ry spe - cial___ time, _____ Shab - bat is a fam - i - ly

C **C7** *To Refrain* 𝄋 **C** **G** **C**

time. _____ 2.On Cha - nu - kah, to - geth— er, ___ - a -

F **G** **C** **F** **Em** **Dm7**

round the shin - ing lights, With games and songs and pres - ents ev - 'ry

Slower

G **C** **F** **C** **G** **C** **G**

night. "Ma - oz tzur y' - shu - a - ti, l' - cha na - eh l' - sha -

A tempo

C **G** **C** **F** **Em** **Dm7** **G**

bei - ach." Cha - nu - kah is a ver - y spe - cial time. _____

F **Em** **Dm7** **Gsus4** **C** **C7** *To Refrain* 𝄋 **C** **G**

Cha - nu - kah is a fam - i - ly time. _____ 3.And at the Pe - sach

C **F** **G** **C** **F** **Em** **Dm7**

Sei - der___ we gath er ev —'ry year, Wait - ing for E - li - jah to ap -

- 35 -

Slower

pear._____ "Dai, dai-ei-nu,___ Dai, dai-ei-nu,___ Dai, dai-ei-nu, Dai-

A tempo

ei-nu, dai-ei-nu." Pe-sach is a ver-y spe-cial time._____

To Refrain

___ Pe-sach is a fam-i-ly time._____

22. OYFN PRIPETCHOK

Words and Music by Mark Warshawsky

אױפֿן פּריפּעטשאָק בּרֶענט אַ
פֵֿײעֶרעל
און אין שטובּ איז הֵײס
און דֶער רֶבּי לֶערֶענט קלֵײנֶע
קינדֶֶערלאַך
דֶעם אַלֶף בֵּית
זֵײטשֶע קינדֶֶערלאַך
גֶעדֶענקטשֶע טײעֶרע
װאָס איהר לֶערֶענט דאָ.
זאָגֶטשֶע נאָך אַמאָל .
און טאַקֶע נאָך אַמאָל
"קמָץ אַלֶף אָ״
בָּרוּךְ אַתָּה יְיָ אֱלֹהֵינוּ מֶלֶךְ הָעוֹלָם
שֶׁהֶחֱיָנוּ וְקִיְּמָנוּ וְהִגִּיעָנוּ לַזְּמַן הַזֶּה.

Oh the fire burns in the fireplace,
And the room is hot.
And the Rabbi teaches all the little boys
The Aleph Bet.
See now the little ones,
Remember children, Don't forget it please.
Say it once and say it over once again.
All your A,B,C's.

23. I'M PROUD TO BE A JEW

Words and Music by Steven Carr Reuben

Refrain:
I'm Proud To Be A Jew.
I'd like for you to know
Whenever I think of who I am
I want to tell you so, because
I'm Proud To Be A Jew.
I'd like for you to know
Whenever I think of who I am
I want to tell you so.

Verse 1
When I am on the playground
It's plain for all to see
I wear a big "Magein David,"
When people look at me, I say:

Refrain

Verse 2
At Pesach time I'm happy
To give my friends a treat
I share the chocolate maccaroons
And Matzah that I eat, because:

Refrain

Verse 3
I'd love to join the choir
And sing out loud and strong.
If they would ask me what I know
I'd sing a Jewish song, I'd sing:

Refrain

Verse 4
If you would like to visit
You'll find me easily,
For on the doorpost of my house
My "mezuzah" you'll see, because:

Refrain

24. THE JEWISH LIFE CYCLE SONG

Words and Music by Julie Jaslow Auerbach

Waltz tempo (♩=132)

Verses

1. A ba - by's born, we wel - come it at
2. The child's thir - teen, a Bar Mitz - vah, and

Syn - a - gogue or at a brit. We con - se - crate our
ab - le to read the To - rah. "Na a - seh v' - nish - ma,"

first grad - ers with Ha - ka - fot and To - rah.
we do con - firm our faith and all that we've learned.

Refrain

For these are Jew - ish lives we live with mile - stones and

hol - i - days. We mark the years as

we grow up in so man - y diff - 'rent ways.

Verse 1
A baby's born, we welcome it
At Synagogue or at a B'rit.
We consecrate our first graders
With Hakafot and Torah.

> **Refrain**
> For these are Jewish lives we live
> With milestones and holidays.
> We mark the years as we grow up
> In so many different ways.

Verse 2
The child's thirteen, a Bar Mitzvah,
And able to read the Torah.
"Na-aseh v'nishma," we do confirm
Our faith and all that we've learned.

> **Refrain**

Verse 3
And when the time has come to wed,
The child is a bride or a groom.
The k'tubah is read, seven blessings are said,
And happiness fills the room.

> **Refrain**

Verse 4
The years go by, a child is born,
And the cycle starts over again.
We give a name and mark the date
And Jewishly celebrate.

> **Refrain**

25. THANK YOU, GOD

Words and Music by Steven Carr Reuben

- 43 -

26. TO SEE THE WORLD
THROUGH JEWISH EYES

Words and Music by Steven Carr Reuben

27. HAYOM YOM HULEDET
Israeli Happy Birthday Song

Folk Song

*Name of Birthday Child

Today is Ya-el's birthday.
Happy Birthday Ya-el!

הַיּוֹם יוֹם הֻלֶּדֶת לְיָעֵל
חַג לָהּ שָׂמֵחַ וְזֵר לָהּ פּוֹרֵחַ
הַיּוֹם יוֹם הֻלֶּדֶת לְיָעֵל

28. ALEF BET SONG*

Words and Music by Debbie Friedman

I.Echo Song. Group repeats each bar.

*Abridged Version

29. BAKITAH*

Words and Music By Debbie Friedman

In the class - room, Ba - ki - tah,___ A boy is "ye - led" and a girl is "yal - dah."___ We call the teach - er "Ha - mo - rah."___ We're learn - ing Heb - rew, "Iv - rit cha - da - shah."___ Mah is "what,"___ Mi is "who,"___ Sha - lom means, "Hi, how do you do?"___ Kein is "Yes,"___ Lo is "No."___ It's fun to sing the words we know.

*Abridged Version

30. B'NI

Proverbs 3: 1-6

Michael Isaacson

- 49 -

My son, do not forget my teaching,
But let your mind retain my commandments;
For they will bestow on you length of days,
Years of life and well-being.
Let fidelity and steadfastness not leave you;
Bind them about your throat,
Write them on the tablet of your mind,
And you will find favor
In the eyes of God and man.
Trust in the Eternal with all your heart,
And do not rely on your own understanding,
In all your ways acknowledge the Eternal,
And God will make your paths smooth.

בְּנִי תּוֹרָתִי אַל-תִּשְׁכָּח
וּמִצְוֹתַי יִצֹּר לִבֶּךָ:
כִּי אֹרֶךְ יָמִים וּשְׁנוֹת חַיִּים
וְשָׁלוֹם יוֹסִיפוּ לָךְ:
חֶסֶד וֶאֱמֶת אַל-יַעַזְבֻךָ
קָשְׁרֵם עַל-גַּרְגְּרוֹתֶיךָ
כָּתְבֵם עַל-לוּחַ לִבֶּךָ:
וּמְצָא-חֵן וְשֵׂכֶל-טוֹב
בְּעֵינֵי אֱלֹהִים וְאָדָם:

בְּטַח אֶל-יְהֹוָה בְּכָל-לִבֶּךָ
וְאֶל-בִּינָתְךָ אַל-תִּשָּׁעֵן:
בְּכָל-דְּרָכֶיךָ דָעֵהוּ
וְהוּא יְיַשֵּׁר אֹרְחֹתֶיךָ:

31. BITI

Words by Kerry Baker   **Music by Michael Isaacson**

בִּתִּי כִּי אַת הַנְּשָׁמָה בֵּנֵינוּ
בִּתִּי כִּי אַת שָׁלוֹם וְשַׁלְוָה
בִּתִּי כִּי אַת הָרוּחַ בְּבֵתֵינוּ
אַתִּי אָת תִּשָׁאֲרִי עַד עוֹלָם
בֹּאִי יַלְדָּה נִלְמַד תּוֹרַת עַמֵּינוּ
בֹּאִי יַלְדָּה נִפְגַּשׁ אֶת הָעוֹלָם
בֹּאִי יַלְדָּה בְּמֶשֶׁךְ כָּל חַיֵּינוּ
נֵלֵךְ אֶל דַּרְכֵי נֹעַם נֹעַם
אָהַבְתִּי יַלְדָּתִי אוֹתָךְ
מִפְּנֵי שֶׁבָּת כִּבְרָכָה אֵל

My daughter, because you are the soul between us,
My daughter, because you are peace and tranquility
My daughter, because you are the spirit of our home
You will remain within our hearts forever.

Come, my child, let us learn the Torah of our people.
Come, my child, let us meet the world.
Come, my child, throughout our lives let us walk in
paths of pleasantness.

We have loved you, our daughter,
For you have brought us blessing.
With tender hands we bless you in return.

My daughter, knowing your love for your parents,
My child, knowing you are the beloved of God,
We give, daughter, our love to you and with it, child, the
blessing of our hearts.

32. AND THE YOUTH SHALL SEE VISIONS

Adapted from Joel 3:1

Debbie Friedman

- 54 -

33. SIMON TOV

Chassidic Song

May good fortune come to us and to all Israel.

סִימָן טוֹב וּמַזָּל טוֹב
יְהֵא לָנוּ וּלְכָל יִשְׂרָאֵל

34. OD YISHAMA

Wedding liturgy

Rabbi S. Carlebach

Again may there be heard in the streets of Judah and in the streets of Jerusalem the voice of gladness, the voice of bridegroom and bride.

עוֹד יִשָּׁמַע בְּעָרֵי יְהוּדָה וּבְחוּצוֹת יְרוּשָׁלַיִם
קוֹל שָׂשׂוֹן וְקוֹל שִׂמְחָה, קוֹל חָתָן וְקוֹל כַּלָּה,

35. EIL MALEI RACHAMIM

Reform Ritual

Traditional Nusach

(lightly)

rei - hu b'- sei - ter k'- na- fav l'- o - la - mim,_____ v' - yitz -
re - ha
reim_____

ror bitz- ror ha- cha- yim et nish - ma - to._____ A - do -
et nish - ma - tah._____
et nish - ma - tam._____

nai hu na - cha - la - to._____ V' - ya -
na - cha - la - tah._____ V' - ta -
na - cha - la - tam._____ V' - ya -

nu - ach b'- sha- lom al mish- ka- vo,_____ v'- no - mar:_____ A- mein._____
nu - ach b'- sha- lom al mish- ka- vah,_____
nu - chu b'- sha- lom al mish- ka- vam,_____

אֵל מָלֵא רַחֲמִים, שׁוֹכֵן בַּמְּרוֹמִים, הַמְצֵא מְנוּחָה
נְכוֹנָה תַּחַת כַּנְפֵי הַשְּׁכִינָה עִם קְדוֹשִׁים וּטְהוֹרִים
כְּזֹהַר הָרָקִיעַ מַזְהִירִים לְנִשְׁמוֹת יַקִּירֵינוּ שֶׁהָלְכוּ
לְעוֹלָמָם. בַּעַל הָרַחֲמִים יַסְתִּירֵם בְּסֵתֶר כְּנָפָיו
לְעוֹלָמִים, וְיִצְרוֹר בִּצְרוֹר הַחַיִּים אֶת־נִשְׁמָתָם. יְיָ
הוּא נַחֲלָתָם. וְיָנוּחוּ בְּשָׁלוֹם עַל מִשְׁכָּבָם, וְנֹאמַר:
אָמֵן.

O God full of compassion, Eternal Spirit of the universe, grant perfect rest under the wings of Your Presence to our loved ones who have entered eternity. God of Mercy, let them find refuge forever in the shadow of Your wings, and let their souls be bound up in the bond of eternal life. The Eternal God is their inheritance. May they rest in peace, and let us say: Amen.

36. THE JEWISH CALENDAR SONG

Words and Music by Julie Jaslow Auerbach

Lively (♩=88)

1. Tish-rei starts the year with Rosh Ha-sha-nah, Yom Kip-pur.——
2. Pe-sach comes, the flow-ers bloom, it's Nis-san, I-yar, Si-van.

De-co-rate your Suk-kah and then march on Sim-chat To-rah.
When it's hot it must be Tam-muz, Av and E-lul.——

Chesh-van, Kis-lev, It's turned cold and time to spin our drei-dels.
It's so nice to cel-e-brate our hol-i-days, so fest-ive.

Here comes spring, it's Te-vet, Sh'vat, A-dar and brave Queen Es-ther.
And our year will start a-gain with Tish-rei, Chesh-van, Kis-lev.

37. SHEHECHEYANU

Traditional Tune

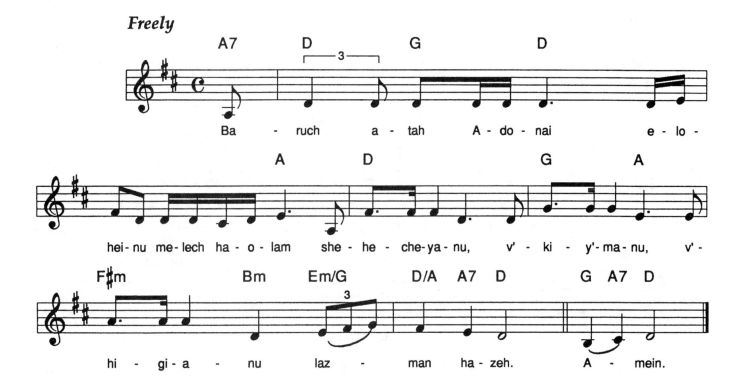

בָּרוּךְ אַתָּה, יְיָ אֱלֹהֵינוּ, מֶלֶךְ הָעוֹלָם, שֶׁהֶחֱיָנוּ וְקִיְמָנוּ
וְהִגִּיעָנוּ לַזְּמַן הַזֶּה.

Blessed is the Eternal our God, Ruler of the universe, for
giving us life, for sustaining us, and for enabling us to
reach this season.

38. SHEHECHEYANU

Tzivika Pik

For translation see #37

39. SHABBAT SHALOM

Nachum Frankel

Welcome Shabbat

שַׁבָּת שָׁלוֹם

40. CHALLAH IN THE OVEN

Raffi

Adapted by Buzz Hellman

41. THE CHALLAH

Words and Music by Julie Jaslow Auerbach

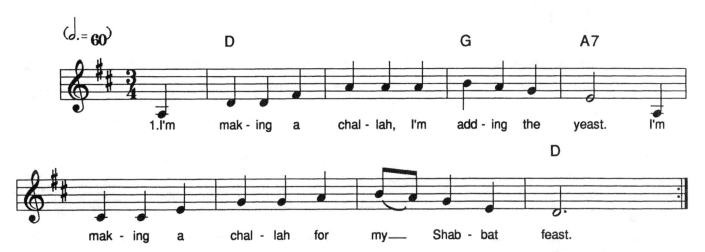

1. I'm mak - ing a chal - lah, I'm add - ing the yeast. I'm

mak - ing a chal - lah for my— Shab - bat feast.

Verse 1
I'm making a challah,
I'm adding the yeast.
I'm making a challah
For my Shabbat feast.

Verse 2
I'm making a challah
With flour and eggs.
I'm making a challah
I'll watch it as it bakes.

Verse 3 *(twisting motions)*
I braid it and twist it
And tuck in the ends.
I braid it and twist it,
It has so many bends.

Verse 4 *(slowly rise)*
I watch as it rises
So slowly at first.
I watch as it rises,
I hope it doesn't burst

Verse 5 *(rise higher and higher)*
Up to the top of the oven it grows.
Up to the top,
Where it stops -
Oh, noone knows!

Verse 6
My challah, my challah,
You're so good to eat.
My challah, my challah,
So warm and fresh and sweet.

42. FRIDAY NIGHT THRU THE NOSE

Words and Music by Leah Abrams

43. ON SHABBAT

Words and Music by Judy Caplan Ginsburgh

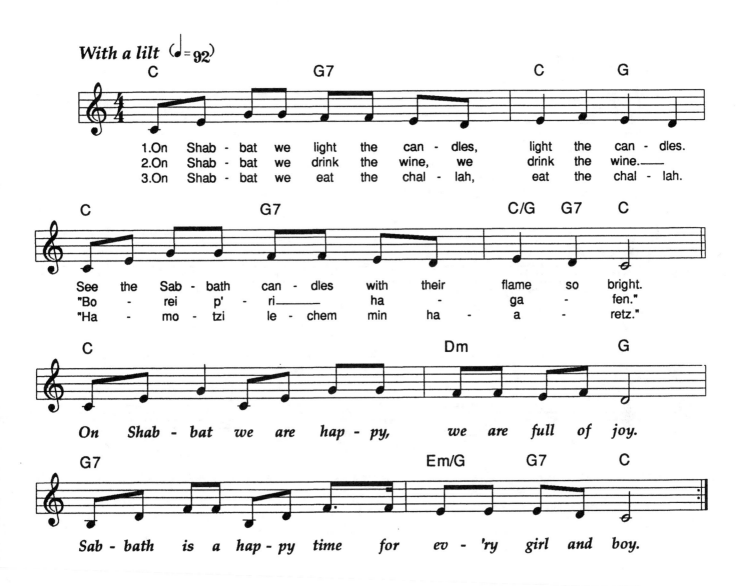

With a lilt (♩=92)

1.On Shab - bat we light the can - dles, light the can - dles.
2.On Shab - bat we drink the wine, we drink the wine.___
3.On Shab - bat we eat the chal - lah, eat the chal - lah.

See the Sab - bath can - dles with their flame so bright.
"Bo - rei p' - ri___ ha - ga - fen."
"Ha - mo - tzi le - chem min ha - a - retz."

On Shab - bat we are hap - py, we are full of joy.

Sab - bath is a hap - py time for ev - 'ry girl and boy.

44. SHABBAT, SHABBAT SHALOM

Words and Music by Julie Jaslow Auerbach

45. STIR THE SOUP

Eve Lippman   **Gladys Gewirtz**

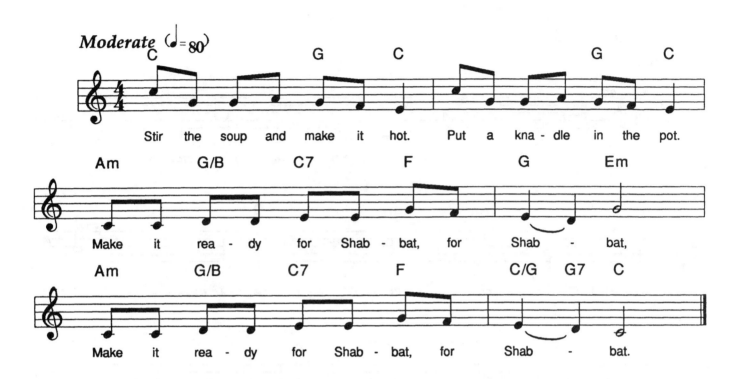

46. L'CHAH DODI

Folk tune

See #47 for complete Hebrew text with English translation.

47. L'CHAH DODI

Liturgy   **Mordechai Zeira**

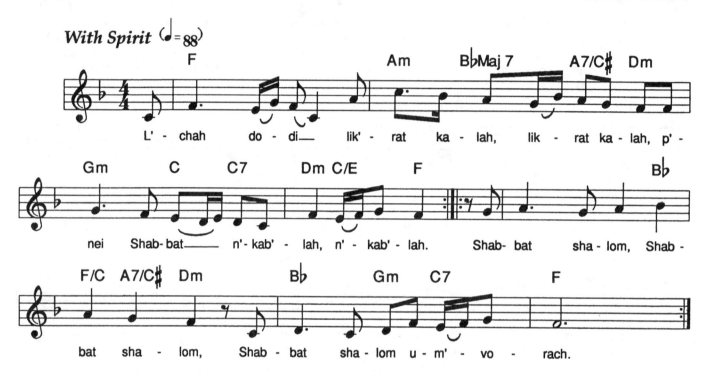

© Copyright by Mifalei Tarbut V'chinuch Edition Israel

Beloved, come to meet the bride; beloved, come to greet Shabbat.

"Keep" and "Remember"; a single command the Only God caused us to hear; the Eternal is One, God's name is One; God's name is honor, glory and praise

Beloved...

Come with me to meet Shabbat, forever a fountain of blessing. Still it flows, as from the start: the last of days, for which the first was made.

Beloved...

Awake, awake, your light has come! Arise, shine, awake and sing: the Eternal's glory dawns upon you.

Beloved...

Enter in peace, O crown of your husband; enter in gladness, enter in joy. Come to the people that keeps its faith. Enter, O bride! Enter, O bride!

Beloved...

לְכָה דוֹדִי לִקְרַאת כַּלָּה פְּנֵי שַׁבָּת נְקַבְּלָה.
לְכָה דוֹדִי לִקְרַאת כַּלָּה פְּנֵי שַׁבָּת נְקַבְּלָה.

שָׁמוֹר וְזָכוֹר בְּדִבּוּר אֶחָד הִשְׁמִיעָנוּ אֵל הַמְיֻחָד.
יְיָ אֶחָד וּשְׁמוֹ אֶחָד לְשֵׁם וּלְתִפְאֶרֶת וְלִתְהִלָּה.
לְכָה ...

לִקְרַאת שַׁבָּת לְכוּ וְנֵלְכָה כִּי הִיא מְקוֹר הַבְּרָכָה.
מֵרֹאשׁ מִקֶּדֶם נְסוּכָה סוֹף מַעֲשֶׂה בְּמַחֲשָׁבָה תְּחִילָה.
לְכָה ...

הִתְעוֹרְרִי הִתְעוֹרְרִי כִּי בָא אוֹרֵךְ! קוּמִי אוֹרִי
עוּרִי עוּרִי שִׁיר דַּבֵּרִי : כְּבוֹד יְיָ עָלַיִךְ נִגְלָה.
לְכָה ...

בּוֹאִי בְשָׁלוֹם עֲטֶרֶת בַּעְלָהּ גַּם בְּשִׂמְחָה וּבְצָהֳלָה
תּוֹךְ אֱמוּנֵי עַם סְגֻלָּה. בּוֹאִי כַלָּה! בּוֹאִי כַלָּה!
לְכָה ...

48. MAH YAFEH HAYOM

Issachar Miron

How lovely is this day of Shabbat peace.

מַה יָפֶה הַיּוֹם שַׁבָּת שָׁלוֹם.

49. SHAVUA TOV
May You Have A Good Week

Lyrics by Jeffrey Klepper and Susan Nanus
Music by Jeffrey Klepper

1.The twist-ed can-dle bright-ens our hearts as to-geth-er we watch the Sab-bath de-part. We smell the spic-es, taste the wine as the stars in the sky be-gin to shine.__ Sha-vu-a tov,__ May you have a good week, May you find the hap-pi-ness you seek.__ Sha-vu-a tov,__ May your week__ be fine, May it be as sweet__ as the Sab-bath wine.

2.We say good-bye__ to a spe-cial friend,__ A-noth-er Shab-bat has come__ to an end. "Sha-vu-a Tov"__ are the words we speak__ To say, "May you have a hap-py week."__ Sha-vu-a tov,__ May you have a good week, May you find the hap-pi-ness you seek.__ Sha-vu-a tov,__ May your week__ be fine, May it ba as sweet__ as the Sab-bath wine.

50. HAMAVDIL - SHAVUA TOV

Folk Song

You separate sacred from profane: separate us now from our failings. Let those who love You be as many as the sands, and as the stars of heaven. May you have a good week.

הַמַּבְדִיל בֵּין קֹדֶשׁ לְחוֹל,

חַטֹּאתֵינוּ הוּא יִמְחֹל,

זַרְעֵנוּ וְכַסְפֵּנוּ יַרְבֶּה כַּחוֹל,

וְכַכּוֹכָבִים בַּלָּיְלָה.

51. CANDLE BLESSING
Shabbat and Festivals

Abraham Wolf Binder

Serene; freely

Ba - ruch a-tah Ado - nai e-lo -hei - nu me-lech ha-o - lam,_____

_____ a - sher ki-d'-sha-nu b'-mitz-vo - tav v'-tzi -

va - nu____ l' - had - lik neir, l' - had - lik

neir shel Shab bat.
shel Shab - bat v' - shel yom_____ tov.
shel yom_____ tov.

Blessed is the Eternal our God, ruler of the universe,
who hallows us with mitzvot, and commands us to
kindle the lights of (Shabbat and) Yom Tov.

בָּרוּךְ אַתָּה יְיָ אֱלֹהֵינוּ מֶלֶךְ הָעוֹלָם
אֲשֶׁר קִדְּשָׁנוּ בְּמִצְוֹתָיו
וְצִוָּנוּ לְהַדְלִיק נֵר
שֶׁל (שַׁבָּת וְשֶׁל) יוֹם טוֹב.

52. SHALOM ALEICHEM

Samuel Goldfarb

שָׁלוֹם עֲלֵיכֶם, מַלְאֲכֵי הַשָּׁרֵת,
מַלְאֲכֵי עֶלְיוֹן,
מִמֶּלֶךְ מַלְכֵי הַמְּלָכִים,
הַקָּדוֹשׁ בָּרוּךְ הוּא.

בּוֹאֲכֶם לְשָׁלוֹם, מַלְאֲכֵי הַשָּׁלוֹם,
מַלְאֲכֵי עֶלְיוֹן,
מִמֶּלֶךְ מַלְכֵי הַמְּלָכִים,
הַקָּדוֹשׁ בָּרוּךְ הוּא.

בָּרְכוּנִי לְשָׁלוֹם, מַלְאֲכֵי הַשָּׁלוֹם,
מַלְאֲכֵי עֶלְיוֹן,
מִמֶּלֶךְ מַלְכֵי הַמְּלָכִים,
הַקָּדוֹשׁ בָּרוּךְ הוּא.

צֵאתְכֶם לְשָׁלוֹם, מַלְאֲכֵי הַשָּׁלוֹם,
מַלְאֲכֵי עֶלְיוֹן,
מִמֶּלֶךְ מַלְכֵי הַמְּלָכִים,
הַקָּדוֹשׁ בָּרוּךְ הוּא.

Peace be to you, O ministering angels, messengers of the
Most High, the supreme Ruler, the Holy One of blessing.
Enter in peace, O messengers of peace...
Bless me with peace, O messengers of peace...
Depart in peace, O messengers of peace...

53. KIDDUSH
Erev Shabbat

Based on
Louis Lewandowski

Freely Moving

Ba - ruch a - tah A - do - nai e - lo - hei - nu me - lech ha - o -

lam bo - rei p' - ri ha - ga - fen. Ba -

ruch a - tah A - do - nai e - lo - hei - nu me - lech ha - o - lam a -

sher ki - d' - sha - nu b'mitz - vo - tav v' - ra - tza va - nu v' - sha -

bat kod - sho b' - a - ha - vah uv - ra - tzon hin - chi - la - nu zi - ka -

ron l' - ma - a - sei v' - rei - shit; ki hu yom t' - chi - lah l' -

בָּרוּךְ אַתָּה יְיָ אֱלֹהֵינוּ מֶלֶךְ הָעוֹלָם
בּוֹרֵא פְּרִי הַגָּפֶן.
בָּרוּךְ אַתָּה יְיָ אֱלֹהֵינוּ מֶלֶךְ הָעוֹלָם
אֲשֶׁר קִדְּשָׁנוּ בְּמִצְוֹתָיו וְרָצָה בָנוּ
וְשַׁבַּת קָדְשׁוֹ בְּאַהֲבָה וּבְרָצוֹן הִנְחִילָנוּ
זִכָּרוֹן לְמַעֲשֵׂה בְרֵאשִׁית.
כִּי הוּא יוֹם תְּחִלָּה לְמִקְרָאֵי קֹדֶשׁ
זֵכֶר לִיצִיאַת מִצְרָיִם.
כִּי־בָנוּ בָחַרְתָּ וְאוֹתָנוּ קִדַּשְׁתָּ מִכָּל־הָעַמִּים
וְשַׁבַּת קָדְשְׁךָ בְּאַהֲבָה וּבְרָצוֹן הִנְחַלְתָּנוּ.
בָּרוּךְ אַתָּה יְיָ מְקַדֵּשׁ הַשַּׁבָּת.

Blessed are You, Eternal God, Ruler of time and space, creator of the fruit of the vine. Blessed are You, Eternal God, Ruler of time and space, who hallows us with Mitzvot and takes delight in us. In Your love and favor You have made Your holy Shabbat our heritage, as a reminder of the work of creation. It is first among our sacred days, and a remembrance of the Exodus from Egypt. O God, You have chosen us and set us apart from all the peoples, and in love and favor have given us the Shabbat as a sacred inheritance. Praised are You, for the Shabbat and its holiness.

54. BIRCHOT HAVDALLAH

Liturgy

Debbie Friedman

בָּרוּךְ אַתָּה יְיָ אֱלֹהֵינוּ מֶלֶךְ הָעוֹלָם
בּוֹרֵא פְּרִי הַגָּפֶן.
בָּרוּךְ אַתָּה יְיָ אֱלֹהֵינוּ מֶלֶךְ הָעוֹלָם
בּוֹרֵא מִינֵי בְשָׂמִים.
בָּרוּךְ אַתָּה יְיָ אֱלֹהֵינוּ מֶלֶךְ הָעוֹלָם
בּוֹרֵא מְאוֹרֵי הָאֵשׁ.

Blessed is the Eternal our God, Ruler of the universe,
Creator of the fruit of the vine.

Blessed is the Eternal our God, Ruler of the universe,
Creator of all the spices.

Blessed is the Eternal our God, Ruler of the universe,
Creator of the light of fire.

55. KI ESHM'RA SHABBAT

Baghdad Folksong

כִּי אֶשְׁמְרָה שַׁבָּת אֵל יִשְׁמְרֵנִי.
אוֹת הִיא לְעוֹלְמֵי עַד בֵּינוֹ וּבֵינִי.

If I keep Shabbat, God watches over me. It is a sign
forever between God and me.

56. TAPUCHIM UD'VASH
Apples and Honey

Israeli Childrens' Song

Apples and honey for the new year.
Apples and honey Rosh Hashana's here!
A very good year, a very sweet year,
Apples and honey for the new year.

תַּפּוּחִים וּדְבָשׁ לְרֹאשׁ הַשָּׁנָה
שָׁנָה טוֹבָה שָׁנָה מְתוּקָה
תַּפּוּחִים וּדְבָשׁ לְרֹאשׁ הַשָּׁנָה

57. SING ALONG SONG

Words and Music by Steven Carr Reuben

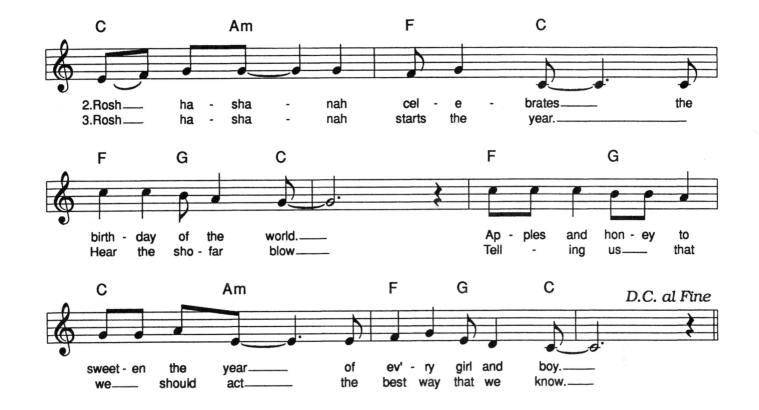

Chorus
Sing along song, come sing along.
Sing along song with me.
It'll make you smile if you sing for a while
This sing along song with me.

1. Woke up this morning feeling fine.
Sang to the morning sun
Let those golden rays pour down
And shine on every one, so they can: **(Chorus)**

2. Rosh Hashanah celebrates
The birthday of the world.
Apples and honey to sweeten the year
Of every girl and boy.   **(Chorus)**

3. Rosh Hashanah starts the year.
Hear the shofar blow
Telling us that we should act
The best way that we know.   **(Chorus)**

4. Yom Kippur reminds us that
It is Atonement Day.
We are sorry for the thoughtless
Words we often say,
Everybody now: **(Chorus)**

5. Yom Kippur's a time when we
Can begin once again.
Go to someone we have hurt
And say, "Come let's be friends."
Everybody now: **(Chorus)**

6. I'm glad you listened to my song.
I hope it made you smile.
Whenever you're down just come around,
We can laugh and sing for awhile,
We can sing my: **(Chorus)**

58. MI CHAMOCHA

High Holy Days

Traditional Tune

Who is like You, Eternal One, among the gods that are worshipped?
Who is like You, majestic in holiness, awesome in splendor, doing wonders?
In their escape from the sea, Your children saw Your sovereign might displayed.
"This is my God!" they cried. "The Eternal will reign for ever and ever!"

מִי־כָמְכָה בָּאֵלִם יְיָ
מִי כָּמְכָה נֶאְדָּר בַּקֹּדֶשׁ
נוֹרָא תְהִלֹּת עֹשֵׂה פֶלֶא
יְיָ יִמְלֹךְ לְעֹלָם וָעֶד

59. L'SHANAH TOVAH

Traditional Tune

Happy New Year! May you be written up in the Book of
Life.

לְשָׁנָה טוֹבָה תִּכָּתֵבוּ

60. AVINU MALKEINU
YOM KIPPUR

Folk Song

Slowly (♩.= 52)

A - vi-nu mal - kei - nu — cha - nei - nu va-a-nei -

nu, — A - vi-nu mal - kei-nu, cha - nei - nu va-a-nei-nu, ki ein ba-nu ma-a -

sim. — A - seih i-ma - nu — tz'- da-kah va-che - sed, — a -

seih i-ma-nu tz' - da-kah va-che - sed v'- ho-shi-ei - nu. —

אָבִינוּ מַלְכֵּנוּ, חָנֵּנוּ וַעֲנֵנוּ, כִּי אֵין בָּנוּ מַעֲשִׂים, עֲשֵׂה
עִמָּנוּ צְדָקָה וָחֶסֶד וְהוֹשִׁיעֵנוּ.

Our Father, our King, be gracious and answer us, for we
have little merit. Treat us generously and with kindness,
and be our help.

61. AVINU MALKEINU

Rosh Hashanah Liturgy

Max Janowski

A - vi - nu Mal - kei - nu sh'-ma____ ko - lei - nu. A - vi - nu Mal - kei - nu cha - ta - nu l'-fa - ne - cha. A - vi - nu Mal - kei - nu cha - mol____ a - lei - nu v' - al____ o - la - lei - nu v' - ta - pei - nu. A - vi - nu Mal - kei - nu ka - leih de - ver v' - che - rev v' - ra - av mei - a - lei - nu. A - vi - nu Mal - kei - nu ka - leih chol____

- 92 -

Our Father, our King, hear our voice.

Our Father, our King, we have sinned against You.

Our Father, our King, have compassion on us and on our children.

Our Father, our King, make an end to sickness, war, and famine.

Our Father, our King, make an end to all oppression.

Our Father, our King, inscribe for blessing in the Book of Life.

Our Father, our King, let the new year be a good year for us.

Our Father, our King, hear our voice.

Our Father, our King, be gracious and answer us, for we have little merit. Treat us generously and with kindness, and be our help.

אָבִינוּ מַלְכֵּנוּ שְׁמַע קוֹלֵנוּ.

אָבִינוּ מַלְכֵּנוּ חָטָאנוּ לְפָנֶיךָ.

אָבִינוּ מַלְכֵּנוּ חֲמוֹל עָלֵינוּ וְעַל עוֹלָלֵינוּ וְטַפֵּנוּ.

אָבִינוּ מַלְכֵּנוּ כַּלֵּה דֶּבֶר וְחֶרֶב וְרָעָב מֵעָלֵינוּ.

אָבִינוּ מַלְכֵּנוּ כַּלֵּה כָל-צַר וּמַשְׂטִין מֵעָלֵינוּ.

אָבִינוּ מַלְכֵּנוּ כָּתְבֵנוּ בְּסֵפֶר חַיִּים טוֹבִים.

אָבִינוּ מַלְכֵּנוּ חַדֵּשׁ עָלֵינוּ שָׁנָה טוֹבָה.

אָבִינוּ מַלְכֵּנוּ שְׁמַע קֹלֵנוּ.

אָבִינוּ מַלְכֵּנוּ חָנֵּנוּ וַעֲנֵנוּ כִּי אֵין בָּנוּ מַעֲשִׂים עֲשֵׂה עִמָּנוּ צְדָקָה וָחֶסֶד וְהוֹשִׁיעֵנוּ.

62. B'YOM KIPPUR

Words and Music by

Linda Tzuroka and Jacqueline Pliskin

On Yom Kippur
The day of fasting
We pray all day
In the synagogue.
God our Ruler
Be gracious to us and answer
Our prayers
On Yom Kippur
The day of fasting
Hear our prayers

בְּיוֹם כִּפּוּר
בְּיוֹם הַצוֹם
בְּבֵית הַכְּנֶסֶת
כֹּל הַיוֹם מִתְפַּלְלִים
אָבִינוּ מַלְכֵנוּ
חָנֵנוּ וַעֲנֵנוּ
בְּיוֹם כִּפּוּר
בְּיוֹם הַצוֹם
שְׁמַע תְּפִלָתֵינוּ

63. KOL NIDREI

Traditional Melodies

- 96 -

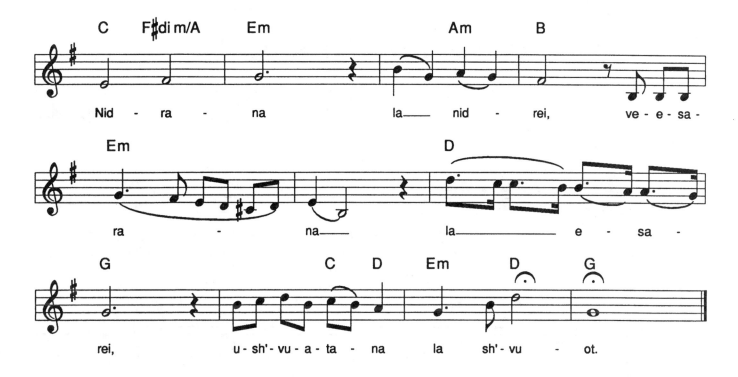

Nid - ra - - - na la__ nid - rei, ve - e - sa -
ra - - na__ la__ e - sa -
rei, u - sh' - vu - a - ta - na la sh' - vu - ot.

כָּל־נִדְרֵי וֶאֱסָרֵי וַחֲרָמֵי וְקוֹנָמֵי וְכִנּוּיֵי וְקִנּוּסֵי
וּשְׁבוּעוֹת, דִּנְדַרְנָא וּדְאִשְׁתְּבַּעְנָא וּדְאַחֲרִימְנָא
וְדַאֲסַרְנָא עַל נַפְשָׁתַנָא, מִיּוֹם כִּפּוּרִים זֶה עַד יוֹם
כִּפּוּרִים הַבָּא עָלֵינוּ לְטוֹבָה, כֻּלְהוֹן אִחֲרַטְנָא בְהוֹן,
כֻּלְהוֹן יְהוֹן שָׁרַן, שְׁבִיקִין שְׁבִיתִין, בְּטֵלִין וּמְבֻטָּלִין,
לָא שְׁרִירִין וְלָא קַיָּמִין. נִדְרַנָא לָא נִדְרֵי, וֶאֱסָרַנָא לָא
אֱסָרֵי, וּשְׁבוּעָתַנָא לָא שְׁבוּעוֹת.

Let all our vows and oaths, all the promises we make and
the obligations we incur to You, O God, between this
Yom Kippur and the next, be null and void should we,
after honest effort, find ourselves unable to fulfill them.
Then may we be forgiven.

64. SUKKOT MORNING

Ray M. Cook

65. THIS IS WHAT WE NEED
TO BUILD A SUKKAH

Words and Music by Debbie Friedman

66. SUKKOT SONG

Words and Music by Steven Carr Reuben

shake to-geth-er lu-lav, ha-das and the a-ra-vah.

Smell the et-rog un-der our Suk-kah.

D.C. al Coda

Coda

You see to the sky, Suk-kot is here.

67. MI CHAMOCHA

Sukkot

Traditional Tune

*For Hebrew and translation
See number 58*

68. TORA LI

Words and Music by Steven Carr Reuben

With a lilt (♩.= 66)

Dance with the To - rah and sing out a song!
To - ra - li, To - ra - li, To - rah she - li!

Dance with the To - rah and sing all day long!
To - ra - li, To - ra - li, To - rah she - li!

To - rah, _____ To - rah she - li. _____
To - vah _____ To - rah she - li. _____

To - rah, To - rah she - li. _____

Verse 3

Boys: Ani samei-ach Girls: Ani sameicha (2x)
All: Tovah Torah sheli.

My Torah
My Torah
Boys (say): I am happy
Girls (say): I am happy

תּוֹרָה לִי
תּוֹרָה שֶׁלִּי
אֲנִי שָׂמֵחַ
אֲנִי שְׂמֵיחָה

69. WHEN WE MARCH ON SIMCHAT TORAH

Words and Music by Debbie Friedman

70. THE DREIDEL SONG

Words and Music by Debbie Friedman

71. IF I WERE A CANDLE

Words and Music by Elaine Serling

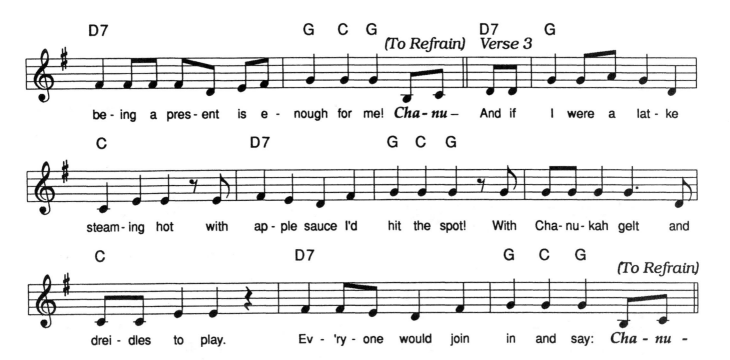

be - ing a pres - ent is e - nough for me! *Cha - nu –* And if I were a lat - ke

steam - ing hot with ap - ple sauce I'd hit the spot! With Cha - nu - kah gelt and

drei - dles to play. Ev - 'ry - one would join in and say: *Cha - nu –*

72. CHANUKAH CANDLE BLESSINGS

Traditional Melody

בָּרוּךְ אַתָּה יְיָ אֱלֹהֵינוּ מֶלֶךְ הָעוֹלָם
אֲשֶׁר קִדְּשָׁנוּ בְּמִצְוֹתָיו
וְצִוָּנוּ לְהַדְלִיק נֵר
שֶׁל חֲנֻכָּה.
בָּרוּךְ אַתָּה יְיָ אֱלֹהֵינוּ מֶלֶךְ הָעוֹלָם
שֶׁעָשָׂה נִסִּים לַאֲבוֹתֵינוּ
בַּיָּמִים הָהֵם בַּזְּמַן הַזֶּה.
בָּרוּךְ אַתָּה יְיָ אֱלֹהֵינוּ מֶלֶךְ הָעוֹלָם
שֶׁהֶחֱיָנוּ וְקִיְּמָנוּ וְהִגִּיעָנוּ לַזְּמַן הַזֶּה.

Blessed is the Eternal our God, Ruler of the universe, by whose Mitzvot we are hallowed, who commands us to kindle the Chanukah lights.

Blessed is the Eternal our God, Ruler of the universe, who performed miracles for our ancestors in days of old, at this season.

Blessed is the Eternal our God, Ruler of the universe, for giving us life, for sustaining us, and for enabling us to reach this season.

73. CHANUKAH

Folk Song

Chanukah is a joyous holiday. Dreidels spin 'round,
candles burn. Oh, let us sing and dance.

חֲנֻכָּה חֲנֻכָּה חַג יָפֶה כָּל כַּךְ.
אוֹר חָבִיב מִסָּבִיב גִּיל לְיֶלֶד רַךְ.
חֲנֻכָּה חֲנֻכָּה סְבִיבוֹן סֹב סֹב
סֹב סֹב סֹב סֹב סֹב סֹב
מַה נָּעִים וָטוֹב.

74. MI CHAMOCHA
Chanukah

Ashkenazic Melody

For Hebrew and translation
See number 58

75. MAOZ TZUR
Rock Of Ages

Hebrew: Mordechai, 13th C.
English: Marcus Jastrow, Gustave Gottheil
Adapted from the German of Leopold Stein

Ashkenazic Melody

Majestically (♩ = 96)

Ma - oz tzur y' - shu - a - ti l' cha na - eh l' - sha-
Rock of a - ges, let our song_____ Praise Your sav - ing_____

bei - ach; Ti - kon beit t' - fi - la - ti v' - sham to - dah n' - za -
pow - er; You, a - mid the rag - ing foes,_____ Were our shel - ter - ing

bei - ach. L'eit ta - chin mat - bei - ach,
tow - er. Fu - rious, they as - sailed us,

mi - tzar ham' - na - bei - ach, Az eg - mor b' -
But Your arm a - vailed_____ us. And Your word_____

shir miz - mor cha - nu - kat ha - miz - bei - ach. bei - ach.
broke their sword,_____ When our own strength failed__ us. failed__ us.

Rock of ages, let our song
Praise Your saving power;
You, amid the raging foes,
Were our sheltering tower.
Furious, they assailed us,
But Your arm availed us,
And Your word
Broke their sword,
When our own strength failed us.

מָעוֹז צוּר יְשׁוּעָתִי,
לְךָ נָאֶה לְשַׁבֵּחַ;
תִּכּוֹן בֵּית תְּפִלָּתִי,
וְשָׁם תּוֹדָה נְזַבֵּחַ.
לְעֵת תָּכִין מַטְבֵּחַ,
מִצָּר הַמְנַבֵּחַ,
אָז אֶגְמוֹר, בְּשִׁיר מִזְמוֹר,
חֲנֻכַּת הַמִּזְבֵּחַ.

76. LIGHT ONE CANDLE

Words and Music by Peter Yarrow

- 115 -

77. CHANUKAH, O CHANUKAH

Folk Song

Chorus

אוֹי חֲנוּכָּה, אוֹי חֲנוּכָּה, אַ יוֹם־טוֹב אַ שֵׁיינער,

אַ לוּסטיקער, אַ פְרֵייילעכער, נישׁטאָנאָך אַזוֹינער.

אַלע נאַכט אִין דְרֵיידְלעך שְׁפִּילן מִיר,

זוּדיק הֵייסע לאַטקעס, עסט אָן אַ שִׁיעוּר.

גֶעשׁוִוינדֶער, צִינדֶט קִינדֶער,

דִי דִינִנְקע לִיכְטעלעך אָן.

זִינגט ״עַל הַנִסִים״, לוֹיבְּט גאָט פֿאַר דִי ״נִסִים״,

אוּן קוּמְט גִיכֶער טאַנצן אִין קאָן.

78. S'VIVON
THE DREIDL

Folk Song

Little dredl, spin, spin, spin. Chanukah is a day of joy.
Great was the miracle that happened there. Spin, little
dredl, spin, spin, spin.

סְבִיבוֹן סֹב סֹב סֹב חֲנֻכָּה הוּא חַג טוֹב!
חֲנֻכָּה הוּא חַג טוֹב! סְבִיבוֹן סֹב סֹב סֹב
חַג שִׂמְחָה הוּא לָעָם נֵס גָּדוֹל הָיָה שָׁם!
נֵס גָּדוֹל הָיָה שָׁם! חַג שִׂמְחָה הוּא לָעָם.

79. MI Y'MALEIL?

Who Can Retell?

English by Judith K. Eisenstein

M. Ravino

* Begin Round

80. LET'S GO PLANT TODAY

Composer unknown
Arranged by Stephen Richards

81. PLANTING SONG

Words and Music by Jeffrey Klepper

seeds will grow and trees will fill the land.
count - ry___ for a tree there's al - ways room! So,
do - ing___ and to - geth - er sing this song!

take a lit - tle seed, Plant it in the___

ground, and that seed will grow___ as the sea-sons flow,___ with

branch - es all a - round,___ And that seed will grow___ as the

sea - sons flow___ with branch - es all a - round.___

82. PURIM GAME

Words and Music by Debbie Friedman

am a Pur - im cook - ie, Yes... a Ha - men - tasch I am!
twirl me round and round and round... a Grog - ger, I make noise!
bout Queen Es - ther and her king... Me -

gi - lah is my name! You guessed what I am, guessed what I am,

You sang nice and loud. You an - swered all the rid - dles, You were

right, now aren't you proud? You right, now aren't you proud?

83. PURIM'S A TIME

Words and Music by Julie Jaslow Auerbach

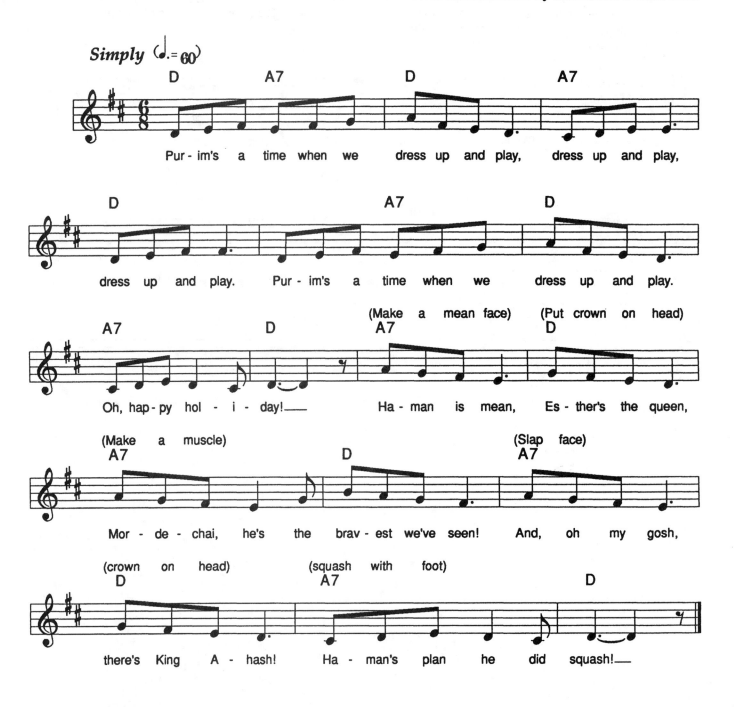

Pur - im's a time when we dress up and play, dress up and play,

dress up and play. Pur - im's a time when we dress up and play.

Oh, hap - py hol - i - day! __ Ha - man is mean, Es - ther's the queen,

Mor - de - chai, he's the brav - est we've seen! And, oh my gosh,

there's King A - hash! Ha - man's plan he did squash! __

84. CHAG PURIM

PURIM DAY

Folk Song

Joyously (♩=84)

Chag Pur - im, Chag Pur - im, Chag ga - dol hu
Pur - im day, Pur - im day, It's a hap - py

la - y'hu - dim. Ma - se - chot ra'a - sha - nim z'mi - rot ri - ku -
hol - i - day. We make noise with our toys, sing and dance and

dim. Ha - vah na - ri - shah rash! rash! rash!
play. Let's hear the grog - gers: rash! rash! rash!

Ha - vah na - ri - shah rash! rash! rash! Ha - vah na - ri - shah
Let's hear the grog - gers: rash! rash! rash! Let's hear the grog - gers:

rash! rash! rash! ba - ra - a - sha - nim.
rash! rash! rash! when they say: "Ha - man!"

חַג פּוּרִים, חַג פּוּרִים, חַג גָּדוֹל הוּא לַיְּהוּדִים,
מַסֵּכוֹת, רַעֲשָׁנִים, זְמִירוֹת, רְקוּדִים.
מַקְהֵלָה:

הָבָה נַרְעִישָׁה, רַשׁ, רַשׁ, רַשׁ,
הָבָה נַרְעִישָׁה, רַשׁ, רַשׁ, רַשׁ,
הָבָה נַרְעִישָׁה, רַשׁ, רַשׁ, בָּרַעֲשָׁנִים.

85. HEY-MAN!
A Purim Reggae

Words and Music by Stephen Richards

Hey, hey, hey, hey, hey, hey, hey, hey - man! Hey, hey, hey,

hey, hey, hey, hey, hey - man! Hey, hey, hey, hey, hey, hey, hey, hey - man!

Hey, hey - man! Hey, Hey - man! Hey, hey -

man!

1. He wan-ted ev'-ry-bo-dy to bow. (Oh wow!) He wan-ted
2. But Mor-dy did-n't know how to bow. (Oh wow!) And Mor-dy

86. YOU CAN CHANGE THE WORLD

Words and Music by

Jeffrey Klepper and Donald Rossoff

With a "Country" Feel (♩ = 104)

1. In a place you may have heard a - bout, in
2. "There's an ev - il plot a - gainst us now, a
3. ___ So Es - ther went be - fore the king, and

Shu - shan, as you know,_____ An ev - il man named
list of cruel de - mands,_____ And Es - ther, on - ly
tho' she was af - raid,_____ She stood up, proud, and

Ha - man said,___ "The Jews have got___ to go."_____ Now,
you can help.___ Our fate is in___ your hands."_____ She said,
spoke out, loud,___ and her peo - ple all___ were saved._____ So

Es - ther was the Jew - ish queen___ and she knew not where to
"Cous - in do you real - ly think___ that a diff - 'rence I can
now we read the Me - gi - lah_____ at Pu - rim time each

turn 'til Mor - de - chai, her cous - in, said,___ "There is
make, a Jew - ish girl be - fore the king,___ It could
year, and learn how God can give us strength_____ to

some-thing you___ must learn. Oh, Es - ther,
be a big___ mis - take." "No, Es - ther,
ov - er - come___ our fear. Re - mem - ber:

You can change___ the

world. You can make the world com - plete.___

Take the pride___ you feel in-side and nev-er ac-cept de-feat."___

87. ESTHER 7: 1, 2

Megilat Esther Chant

Free chant

1.Va - ya - vo ha - me - lech v' - Ha - man lish - tot im Es - ter ha - mal - kah. 2.Va - yo - mer ha - me - lech l' - Es - ter gam ba - yom ha - shei - ni b' - mish - teih ha - ya - yin, mah sh' - ei - la - teich, Es - ter ha - mal - kah v' - ti - na - ten lach; u - mah ba - ka - sha - teich ad cha - tzi ha - mal - chut v' - tei - as.

So the king and Haman came to feast with Queen Esther. Again, the king said to Esther on the second day of the banquet of wine: "What is your petition, Queen Esther? It will be granted to you. What is your request? Even if it is half the kingdom, it will be done."

וַיָּבֹא הַמֶּלֶךְ וְהָמָן לִשְׁתּוֹת עִם־אֶסְתֵּר הַמַּלְכָּה:
וַיֹּאמֶר הַמֶּלֶךְ לְאֶסְתֵּר גַּם בַּיּוֹם הַשֵּׁנִי בְּמִשְׁתֵּה הַיַּיִן
מַה־שְּׁאֵלָתֵךְ אֶסְתֵּר הַמַּלְכָּה וְתִנָּתֵן לָךְ
וּמַה־בַּקָּשָׁתֵךְ עַד־חֲצִי הַמַּלְכוּת וְתֵעָשׂ.

88. PESACH IS HERE TODAY

Words and Music by Steven Carr Reuben

89. SEDER TABLE

Words and Music by Debbie Friedman

90. THE SEDER PLATE SONG

Words and Music by Barbara Bar-Nissim

Calypso (♩ = 116)

On Pass-o - ver we cel- e - brate— by set-ting out a Se- der plate.— On it we put sev-en things— to re-mem- ber Jew-ish hap-pen - ings.— On it we put sev-en things— to re- mem- ber Jew - ish hap-pen - ings.—

Pars-ley stands for spring, salt wat - er for the slaves' tears, cha - ro - set for the mor - tar, bit - ter

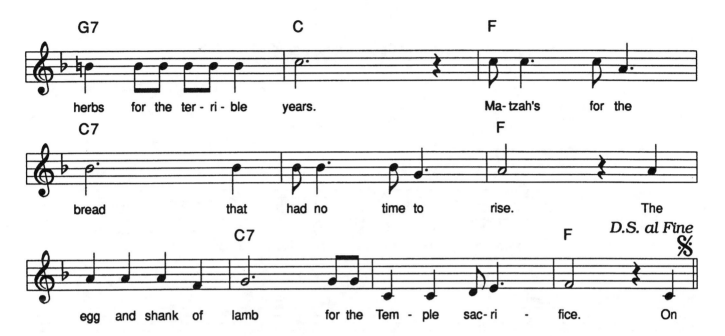

herbs for the ter-ri-ble years. Ma-tzah's for the bread that had no time to rise. The egg and shank of lamb for the Tem-ple sac-ri-fice. On

91. I AM THE AFIKOMEN

Words and Music by Debbie Friedman

92. CHAROSET RECIPE SONG

Words and Music by Nili Rabinovitz

93. KAREIV YOM

Haggadah   **Folk tune**

Bring near the day that is neither day nor night.
Declare Most High, that the day is Yours, and Yours the night.
Place guards over Your city all the day and all the night.
Make bright as the light of day the darkness of the night.

קָרֵב יוֹם אֲשֶׁר הוּא לֹא יוֹם
וְלֹא לַיְלָה.
רָם הוֹדַע כִּי לְךָ הַיּוֹם
אַף לְךָ הַלַּיְלָה.
שׁוֹמְרִים הַפְקֵד לְעִירְךָ
כָּל־הַיּוֹם וְכָל־הַלַּיְלָה.
תָּאִיר כְּאוֹר יוֹם חֶשְׁכַת לַיְלָה.

94. DAYEINU

Folk Song

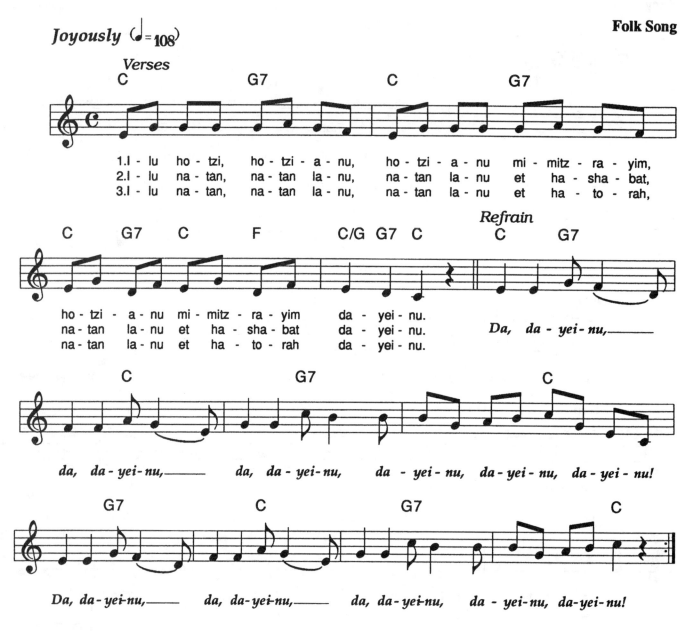

Had God brought us out of Egypt and not supported us
in the wilderness–
It would have been enough!
Had God given us the Sabbath and not the Torah–
It would have been enough!
Had God given us the Torah and not brought us to the
land of Israel–
It would have been enough!

אִלוּ הוֹצִיאָנוּ מִמִּצְרַיִם

דַּיֵּנוּ!

אִלוּ נָתַן לָנוּ אֶת-הַשַּׁבָּת

וְלֹא נָתַן לָנוּ אֶת-הַתּוֹרָה-

דַּיֵּנוּ!

אִלוּ נָתַן לָנוּ אֶת-הַתּוֹרָה

וְלֹא הִכְנִיסָנוּ לְאֶרֶץ יִשְׂרָאֵל-

דַּיֵּנוּ!

95. ADIR HU

God Of Might

Traditional tune

God of Might, God of right,
We would bow before You,
Sing Your praise in these days,
Celebrate Your glory,
As we hear, year by year,
Freedom's wondrous story.

אַדִּיר הוּא. אַדִּיר הוּא. יִבְנֶה בֵיתוֹ
בְּקָרוֹב. בִּמְהֵרָה. בִּמְהֵרָה. בְּיָמֵינוּ
בְּקָרוֹב. אֵל בְּנֵה. אֵל בְּנֵה. בְּנֵה
בֵיתְךָ בְּקָרוֹב:

96. MI CHAMOCHA
Passover

Traditional "Adir Hu" Tune

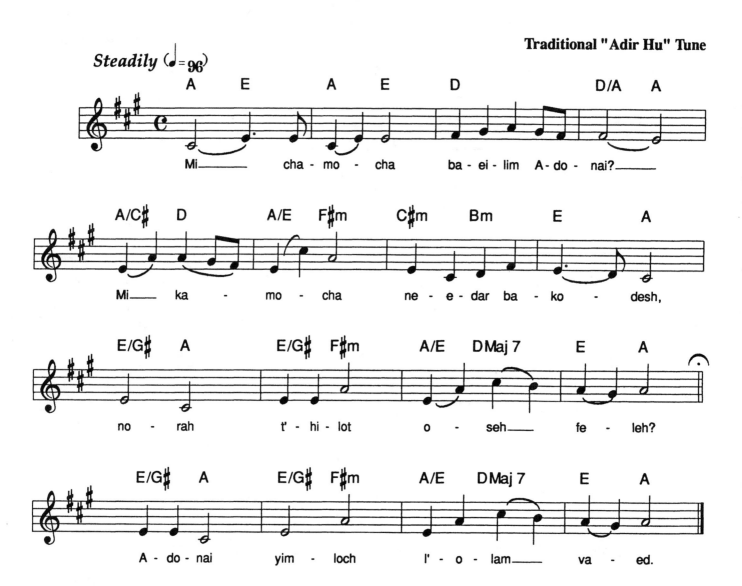

For Hebrew and translation
See number 58

97. THE BALLAD OF THE FOUR SONS

(Tune of "Clementine")

Folk Song

Moving (♩=96)

E

Said the fath - er to his child - ren, "At the
fath - er had no daugh - ters, But his

B   F#m   B7

Sed - er you will dine, You will eat your fill of
sons, they num - bered four. One was wise and one was

E   B   1. thru 10. E   Last verse

Mat - zah, You will drink four cups of wine." Now this four.
wick - ed, One was sim - ple and a bore. And the

1. Said the father to his children,
At the Seder you will dine,
You will eat your fill of matzah,
You will drink four cups of wine."

2. Now this father had no daughters,
But his sons, they numbered four.
One was wise and one was wicked,
One was simple and a bore.

3. And the fourth was sweet and winsome,
He was young and he was small.
While his brothers asked the questions
He could scarcely speak at all.

4. Said the wise son to his father,
"Would you please explain the laws
Of the customs of the Seder;
Will you please explain the cause?"

5. And the father proudly answered,
"As our fathers ate in speed,
Ate the Paschal lamb 'ere midnight
And from slavery were freed."

6. "So we follow their example
And 'ere midnight must complete
All the Seder; and we should not
After twelve remain to eat."

7. Then did sneer the son so wicked,
"What does all this mean to you?"
And the father's voice was bitter
As his grief and anger grew.

8. If yourself you don't consider
As a son of Israel,
Then for you this has no meaning,
You could be a slave as well."

9. Then the simple son said softly,
"What is this?" and quietly
The good father told his offspring
"We were freed from slavery."

10. But the youngest son was silent
For he could not ask at all.
And his eyes were bright with wonder
As his father told him all.

11. Now, dear children, heed the lesson
And remember ever more
What the father told his children,
Told his sons that numbered four.

98. CHAD GADYA
AN ONLY KID

Folk Song

Lively; varying tempi

C G C G C G C G
burned the stick that— beat the dog that— bit the cat— that— ate the kid my—
C G7/D C/E C G7/D C/E F C/G G7
fath - er bought for two——— zu - zim. Chad gad - ya,——— chad gad -
C a tempo G7/D C/E accel. C G
ya. Then— came the but-cher and slew— the— ox that— drank the wat-er that—
C G C G C G C G
quenched the fire that— burned the stick that— beat the dog that— bit the cat that—
C G C G7/D C/E C G7/D C/E F
ate the kid my— fath-er bought for two——— zu-zim. Chad gad - ya,———
Slower; solemn
Faster and faster...
C/GG7 C G7 C G
chad gad -ya. Then— came the an-gel of death, and— killed the but-cher that—
C G C G C G
slew the ox that— drank the wat-er that— quenched the fire that—
C G C G C G C G
burned the stick that— beat the dog that— bit the cat that— ate the kid my—

- 147 -

My father bought for two *zuzim chad gadya.*

חַד גַּדְיָא, חַד גַּדְיָא,
דְּזַבַּן אַבָּא בִּתְרֵי זוּזֵי;
חַד גַּדְיָא, חַד גַּדְיָא,

99. KADEISH UR'CHATZ
The Order Of The Seider

Babylonian Tune

Ka-deish___ u - r'- chatz kar - pas___ ya - chatz

ma - gid___ roch - tza mo - tzi___ ma - tza

ma - ror___ ko - reich shul - chan___ o - reich

tza - fun___ ba - reich ha - leil___ nir - tza

1. Sanctify the Name of God (Kiddush)　　　קַדֵּשׁ

2. Wash the Hands　　　וּרְחַץ

3. Eat the Green Vegetable　　　כַּרְפַּס

4. Break the Middle of Three Matzot　　　יַחַץ

5. Tell the Story of the Exodus　　　מַגִּיד

6. Wash Hands Before the Meal　　　רָחְצָה

7. Say Ha-Motzi　　　מוֹצִיא

8. Recite Blessing for the Matzah　　　מַצָּה

9. Eat Bitter Herbs (Dipped in Ḥaroset)　　　מָרוֹר

10. Eat Matzah and Maror Sandwich　　　כּוֹרֵךְ

11. Enjoy the Festival Meal　　　שֻׁלְחָן עוֹרֵךְ

12. Eat the Afikoman　　　צָפוּן

13. Recite Birkat Hamazon (Grace)　　　בָּרֵךְ

14. Recite the Hallel (Second Part)　　　הַלֵּל

15. Conclude the Seder　　　נִרְצָה

100. EILIYAHU HANAVI

Folk Song

Ei - li - ya - hu ha - na - vi, Ei - li - ya - hu ha - tish-

bi, Ei - li - ya - hu, Ei - li - ya - hu, Ei - li - ya - hu ha gi - la-

di. Bim'- hei - ra b' - ya - mei - nu ya - vo———— ei -

lei - nu im ma - shi - ach ben da - vid, im ma - shi - ach ben da - vid.

Elijah the prophet
In Elijah we will rejoice
May the day come quickly,
When the Messiah will come,
The descendant of King David

אֵלִיָּהוּ הַנָּבִיא, אֵלִיָּהוּ הַתִּשְׁבִּי,
אֵלִיָּהוּ, אֵלִיָּהוּ, אֵלִיָּהוּ הַגִּלְעָדִי,
בִּמְהֵרָה בְיָמֵינוּ יָבֹא אֵלֵינוּ
עִם מָשִׁיחַ בֶּן דָּוִד, עִם מָשִׁיחַ בֶּן דָּוִד.

101. GO DOWN, MOSES!

Spiritual

When Is - rael was in E - gypt land, "Let my peo-ple go!" Op - pressed so hard they could not stand, "Let my peo-ple go!" Go down, Mo - ses, Way down in E - gypt land,— Tell— old Pha - raoh— "Let my peo-ple go!"

102. MAH NISHTANAH?

Adapted From Traditional Haggadah

Debbie Friedman

all oth - er nights — we eat all kinds of herbs, — but on this night the bit - ter one we

bite. On all oth - er nights — we don't dip our food, — but on

this night — we dip it twice. On all oth - er nights — we sit up

straight in our chairs, — but on this night we lean, — and it's nice!

Coda

Mah nish - ta - nah — ha - lai - lah ha - zeh — mi - kol

ha - lei - lot? _____

103. MAH NISHTANAH
The Four Questions

Israeli tune

מַה נִּשְׁתַּנָּה הַלַּיְלָה הַזֶּה מִכָּל הַלֵּילוֹת.
שֶׁבְּכָל הַלֵּילוֹת אָנוּ אוֹכְלִין חָמֵץ וּמַצָּה, הַלַּיְלָה הַזֶּה כֻּלּוֹ מַצָּה.
שֶׁבְּכָל הַלֵּילוֹת אָנוּ אוֹכְלִין שְׁאָר יְרָקוֹת, הַלַּיְלָה הַזֶּה מָרוֹר.
שֶׁבְּכָל הַלֵּילוֹת אֵין אָנוּ מַטְבִּילִין אֲפִילוּ פַּעַם אֶחָת, הַלַּיְלָה הַזֶּה שְׁתֵּי פְעָמִים.
שֶׁבְּכָל הַלֵּילוֹת אָנוּ אוֹכְלִין בֵּין יוֹשְׁבִין וּבֵין מְסֻבִּין, הַלַּיְלָה הַזֶּה כֻּלָּנוּ מְסֻבִּין.

Why is this night different from all the other nights?
On all other nights, we eat either leavened bread or
matzah; on this night–only matzah.
On all other nights, we eat all kinds of herbs; on this
night, we especially eat bitter herbs.
On all other nights, we do not dip herbs at all; on this
night we dip them twice.
On all other nights, we eat in an ordinary manner;
tonight we dine with special ceremony.

104. MAH NISHTANAH
The Four Questions

Traditional Haggadah Chant

For Hebrew and translation
See number 103

105. AVADIM HAYINU

Once We Were Slaves, Now We Are Free!

S. Postolsky

Bright ♩=120

Dm — Gm — A7 — Dm — Gm

A - va - dim ha - yi - nu, ha - yi - nu a - tah b' - nei cho - rin___ b' -

A7 — Dm — F — Gm — Dm

nei cho - rin. A - va - dim___ ha - yi - nu a -

G. — Gm — Dm — F

tah, a - tah b' - nei cho - rin___ a - va - dim___

Dm — Gm — A7 — Dm

ha - yi - nu a - tah, a - tah b' - nei cho - rin, b' - nei cho - rin.

Once we were slaves. Today we are free.

עֲבָדִים הָיִינוּ, עַתָּה בְּנֵי חוֹרִין.

106. HA LACHMA ANYA
This Is The Bread Of Affliction

Emanuel Pugatchev

הָא לַחְמָא עַנְיָא דִּי אֲכָלוּ אַבָהָתָנָא בְּאַרְעָא דְּמִצְרָיִם. כָּל־דִּכְפִין יֵיתֵי וְיֵכֻל. כָּל־דִּצְרִיךְ יֵיתֵי וְיִפְסַח. הָשַׁתָּא הָכָא. לְשָׁנָה הַבָּאָה בְּאַרְעָא דְיִשְׂרָאֵל. הָשַׁתָּא עַבְדֵי. לְשָׁנָה הַבָּאָה בְּנֵי חוֹרִין:

This is the bread of affliction,
the poor bread,
which our ancestors ate in the land of Egypt.
Let all who are hungry come and eat.
Let all who are in want
share the hope of Passover.
As we celebrate here,
we join with our people everywhere.
This year we celebrate here.
Next year in the land of Israel.
Now we are all still in bonds.
Next year may all be free.

107. ECHAD MI YODEI'A
Who Knows One?

Folk Song

Who knows one? I know one.
One is our God, in heaven and on earth.

Who knows two? I know two.
Two are the tablets of the commandments;
One is our God, in heaven and on earth.

אֶחָד מִי יוֹדֵעַ, אֶחָד אֲנִי יוֹדֵעַ:
אֶחָד אֱלֹהֵינוּ שֶׁבַּשָּׁמַיִם וּבָאָרֶץ.

שְׁנַיִם מִי יוֹדֵעַ, שְׁנַיִם אֲנִי יוֹדֵעַ:
שְׁנֵי לֻחוֹת הַבְּרִית,
אֶחָד אֱלֹהֵינוּ שֶׁבַּשָּׁמַיִם וּבָאָרֶץ.

108. ZOG NIT KEYNMOL
Song of the Partisans

Words by Hirsh Glik

Adapted from a melody by Pokras

זאָג ניט קיינמאָל אַז דו גייסט דעם לעצטן וועג,
ווען הימלען בלייענע פאַרשטעלן בלויע טעג.
ווייל קומען וועט נאָך אונדזער אויסגעבענקטע שעה,
ס׳וועט אַ פויק טאָן אונדזער טראָט: מיר זײַנען דאָ!

פון גרינעם פאַלמען־לאַנד ביז ווייסן לאַנד פון שניי,
מיר זײַנען דאָ, מיט אונדזער פּיין, מיט אונדזער וויי.
און וווּ געפאַלן ס׳איז אַ שפּריץ פון אונדזער בלוט,
וועט אַ שפּראָץ טאָן אונדזער גבורה, אונדזער מוט.

You must not say that you now walk the final way,
Because the darkened heavens hide the blue of day.
The time we've longed for will at least draw near,
And our steps, as drums, will sound that we are here.

From land all green with palms, to lands all white with snow
We now arrive with all our pain and woe.
Where our blood sprayed out and came to touch the land,
There our courage and our faith will rise and stand.

109. THE LAST BUTTERFLY

Pavel Freedman   Lisa Glatzer Shenson

*The poet died in the Terezin Concentration Camp
at the age of fourteen.*

110. ANI MA'AMIN

Moses Maimonides

Folk Song
Arranged by Stephen Richards

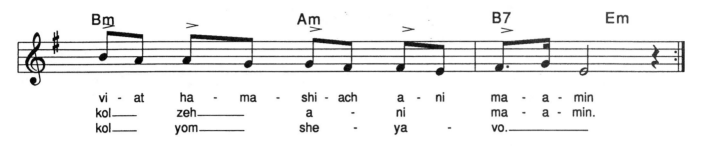

vi - at ha - ma - shi - ach a - ni ma - a - min
kol____ zeh____ a - ni ma - a - min.
kol____ yom____ she - ya - vo.____

Coda

A - ni ma - a- min, a - ni ma - a- min, a - ni__ ma - a -

min, a - ni__ ma - a - min.

I believe with perfect faith in the Messiah's coming. And even if the Messiah be late, I will still wait.

אֲנִי מַאֲמִין בֶּאֱמוּנָה שְׁלֵמָה
בְּבִיאַת הַמָּשִׁיחַ.
וְאַף עַל פִּי שֶׁיִּתְמַהְמֵהַּ
עִם כָּל זֶה אֲנִי מַאֲמִין
עִם כָּל זֶה אֲחַכֶּה לוֹ
בְּכָל יוֹם שֶׁיָּבוֹא.

111. ASHREI HAGAFRUR
Blessed Is The Match

Words by Hannah Szenesh
English verse by Lawrence Avery

Music by Lawrence Avery

Blessed is the match consumed in kindling flame.
Blessed is the flame that burns in the heart's secret places.
Blessed is the heart with strength to stop its beating for honor's sake.
Blessed is the match consumed in kindling flame.

אַשְׁרֵי הַגַּפְרוּר שֶׁנִּשְׂרַף וְהִצִּית לֶהָבוֹת.
אַשְׁרֵי הַלֶּהָבָה שֶׁבָּעֲרָה בְּסִתְרֵי לְבָבוֹת.
אַשְׁרֵי הַלְּבָבוֹת שֶׁיָּדְעוּ לַחֲדֹל בְּכָבוֹד.
אַשְׁרֵי הַגַּפְרוּר שֶׁנִּשְׂרַף וְהִצִּית לֶהָבוֹת.

112. BIRDSONG

Anonymous

Raymond Smolover

From the Terezin Concentration Camp; 1942-1944

Pensively soft and unhurried

1. He does-n't know the world at all,____ Who stays____ in his nest and won't come out. He does-n't know what birds know best, Nor what I want to sing a-bout, What I want to sing a-bout, What I want to sing a-bout, is that the world is full of love-li-ness.

2. When dew-drops spark-le in the grass,____ And earth's a-flood with morn-ing light____ A black-bird sings up-on a bush To greet the dawn-ing aft-er night, To greet the dawn-ing af-ter night, to greet the dawn-ing af-ter night, Then I know how good it is to be a-live.

3. O-pen up your heart to beau-ty, And go____ to the woods some day.____ And weave a wreathe of mem'-ries there And if the tears ob-scure your way; If the tears ob-scure your way, If the tears ob-scure your way, you will know how good it is to be a-live.

113. ZUM GALI, GALI
Round

Second Verse by Harry Coopersmith

Folk Song

The pioneer is for the sake of work.
Work is for the sake of the pioneer.

זוּם גַּלִי גַּלִי גַּלִי
זוּם גַּלִי גַּלִי
הֶחָלוּץ לְמַעַן עֲבוֹדָה
עֲבוֹדָה לְמַעַן הֶחָלוּץ
זוּם...

114. KUM BACHUR ATZEIL

Folk Song

Get up, get up, lazy youth, and go out to work.
Get up, get up, and go to work.
Kukuriku, kukuriku, the rooster crowed.

קוּם בָּחוּר עָצֵל וְצֵא לַעֲבוֹדָה
קוּם קוּם וְצֵא לַעֲבוֹדָה
קוּקוּרִיקוּ קוּקוּרִיקוּ הַתַּרְנְגוֹל קָרָא.

115. EREV SHEL SHOSHANIM
Evening Of The Roses

Moshe Dor   Yosef Hadar

An evening fragrant with roses.
Let us go out to the orchard.
Myrrh, spices and frankincense shall be as a threshold
for your feet.

עֶרֶב שֶׁל שׁוֹשַׁנִּים נֵצֵא נָא אֶל הַבֻּסְתָּן
מוֹר בְּשָׂמִים וּלְבֹנָה לְרַגְלֵךְ מִפְתָּן
לַיְלָה יוֹרֵד לְאַט וְרוּחַ שׁוֹשָׁן נוֹשְׁבָה
הָבָה אֶלְחַשׁ לָךְ שִׁיר בַּלָּאט, זֶמֶר שֶׁל אַהֲבָה
שַׁחַר הוֹמָה יוֹנָה רֹאשֵׁךְ מָלֵא טְלָלִים
פִּיךְ אֶל הַבֹּקֶר שׁוֹשַׁנָה אֶקְטְפֶנּוּ לִי...

116. MAYIM, MAYIM
Water Dance

Isaiah

Emanuel Amiran

Joyfully shall you draw upon the wells of redemption.

וּשְׁאַבְתֶּם מַיִם בְּשָׂשׂוֹן
מִמַּעַיְנֵי הַיְשׁוּעָה

117. SHIR BABOKER BABOKER

Amir Gilboa

Shlomo Artzi and Gideon Koren

Suddenly the people arise in the morning and feel they
are a nation.
To whomever they meet they call out shalom.

פִּתְאֹם קָם אָדָם בַּבֹּקֶר
וּמַרְגִּישׁ כִּי הוּא עָם וּמַתְחִיל לָלֶכֶת
וּלְכָל הַנִּפְגָּשׁ בְּדַרְכּוֹ קוֹרֵא הוּא שָׁלוֹם
דְּגָנִים עוֹלִים מוּל פָּנָיו מִבֵּן חָרִיצֵי הַמִּדְרֶכֶת
וְנִיחוֹחוֹת לְרֹאשׁוֹ מַדִּיפִים עֲצֵי אֲזַדְרֶכֶת
הַטְּלָלִים רוֹסְסִים וְהָרִים רְבוֹא קַרְנַיִם
הֵם יוֹלִידוּ חוּפַּת שֶׁמֶשׁ לִכְלוּלוֹתָיו

118. IM TIRTZU
If You Will It, It Is No Dream

Words from Theodore Herzl and N.H. Imber

Debbie Friedman

© Copyright 1976 by the Composer

If you will it, it is no legend
to be a free people in our land
in Zion and Jerusalem.

לִהְיוֹת עַם חוֹפְשִׁי בְּאַרְצֵנוּ
בְּאֶרֶץ צִיּוֹן וִירוּשָׁלָיִם.

אִם תִּרְצוּ
אֵין זוֹ אַגָּדָה

119. KACHOL V'LAVAN
The Blue And The White

I. Reshel

Russian Folk Song

Blue and white—these are my colors, the colors of my land.
Blue and white—these shall be my colors all the days of my life, forever.

כָּחוֹל וְלָבָן זֶה צֶבַע שֶׁלִי. כָּחוֹל וְלָבָן
כָּחוֹל וְלָבָן צִבְעֵי אַדְמָתִי. זֶה צֶבַע שֶׁלִי כָּל יְמֵי לְעוֹלָם.

120. SISU ET Y'RUSHALAYIM

Isaiah 66:10

Akiva Nof

Rejoice with Jerusalem all you who love her. I have set guards upon thy walls O, Jerusalem. They shall never hold their peace, day or night.

א. שִׂישׂוּ אֶת יְרוּשָׁלַיִם גִּילוּ בָהּ
גִּילוּ בָהּ כָּל אֹהֲבֶיהָ כָּל אֹהֲבֶיהָ

ב. עַל חוֹמוֹתַיִךְ עִיר דָּוִד הִפְקַדְתִּי שׁוֹמְרִים
כָּל הַיּוֹם וְכָל הַלַּיְלָה... (שִׂישׂוּ).

121. Y'RUSHALAYIM

Avigdor Hameiri

Anonymous

מֵעַל פִּסְגַת הַר הַצּוֹפִים
אֶשְׁתַּחֲוֶה לָךְ אַפָּיִם
מֵעַל פִּסְגַת הַר הַצּוֹפִים
שָׁלוֹם לָךְ יְרוּשָׁלַיִם!
מֵאָה דוֹרוֹת חָלַמְתִּי עָלַיִךְ
לִזְכּוֹת לִרְאוֹת בְּאוֹר פָּנַיִךְ
יְרוּשָׁלַיִם יְרוּשָׁלַיִם
הָאִירִי פָּנַיִךְ לִבְנֵךְ
יְרוּשָׁלַיִם יְרוּשָׁלַיִם
מֵחָרְבוֹתַיִךְ אֶבְנֵךְ

From atop Mount Scopus we greet you, O Jerusalem. For
a hundred generations we dreamed of your beauty.
Jerusalem, we shall once again rebuild you.

122. LACH Y'RUSHALAYIM

Amos Etinger   **Eli Rubenstein**

ב. לָךְ יְרוּשָׁלַיִם לָךְ קְדוּמִים וָהוֹד
לָךְ יְרוּשָׁלַיִם לָךְ רָזִים וָסוֹד...

א. לָךְ יְרוּשָׁלַיִם בֵּין חוֹמוֹת הָעִיר
לָךְ יְרוּשָׁלַיִם אוֹר חָדָשׁ יָאִיר

ג. לָךְ יְרוּשָׁלַיִם שִׁיר נִשָּׂא תָּמִיד
לָךְ יְרוּשָׁלַיִם עִיר מִגְדַּל דָּוִד

פזמון
בְּלִבֵּנוּ רַק שִׁיר אֶחָד קַיָם
לָךְ יְרוּשָׁלַיִם בֵּין יַרְדֵּן וָיָם

For you, O Jerusalem, fortress of King David, let a new
light shine
In our hearts there exists but one song, a song dedicated
to you.

123. HATIKVAH

N. H. Imber

Folk Themes

As long as a Jewish heart beats,
and as long as Jewish eyes look eastward,
then our two thousand year hope
to be a free nation in Zion is not dead.

עוֹד לֹא אָבְדָה תִּקְוָתֵנוּ
הַתִּקְוָה בַּת שְׁנוֹת אַלְפַּיִם
לִהְיוֹת עַם חָפְשִׁי בְּאַרְצֵנוּ
אֶרֶץ צִיוֹן וִירוּשָׁלַיִם

כָּל עוֹד בַּלֵּבָב פְּנִימָה
נֶפֶשׁ יְהוּדִי הוֹמִיָּה
וּלְפַאֲתֵי מִזְרָח קָדִימָה
עַיִן לְצִיוֹן צוֹפִיָּה

124. SHAVUOT

Words and Music by Steven Carr Reuben

Shavuot, the time of the Giving of Torah
Shavuot, the holiday of the offerings.

שָׁבוּעוֹת זְמַן מַתָּן תּוֹרָתֵנוּ
חַג הַבִּיקוּרִים.

125. YISRAEIL V'ORAITA

Folk Song

Israel and the Torah and the Blessed are one.
The Torah is light; Halleluyah.

יִשְׂרָאֵל וְאוֹרַיְתָא וְקֻדְשָׁא
בְּרִיךְ הוּא חַד הוּא.
תּוֹרָה אוֹרָה, תּוֹרָה אוֹרָה, הַלְלוּיָה.

126. MI CHAMOCHA
Shavuot

Traditional

For Hebrew and translation
See number 58

127. THE SYNAGOGUE

Words by Jeffrey Klepper and Susan Nanus   **Music by Jeffrey Klepper**

1.In the syn - a - gogue we cel - e - brate just
2.In the syn - a - gogue on Fri - day night we
3.In the syn - a - gogue we stu - dy and learn a -

like a fam - i - ly. On ev - 'ry Jew - ish
greet the Sab - bath bride. A spe - cial kind of
bout our Jew - ish past. The syn - a - gogue is the

hol - i - day it's the place where you should be.
hol - i - ness is on - ly found in - side.
kind of place we know will al - ways last.

Beit k' - nes - et: House of meet - ing. Beit t'fi - lah:

House of prayer. Beit mid - rash: House of stu - dy.

Jew-ish life is hap-pen-ing there, The syn-a - gogue is where!

128. MEZUZAH

Words by Jeffrey Klepper and Susan Nanus

Music by Jeffrey Klepper

129. MENORAH

Words and Music by Jeffrey Klepper

130. KIPAH

Words by Jeffrey Klepper and Susan Nanus

Music by Jeffrey Klepper

131. HANDS HOLD THE TORAH

Words and Music by Steven Carr Reuben

132. THE PEOPLE IN MY SYNAGOGUE

Based on "The People In Your Neighborhood"
by Jeffrey Moss
Adaptation by Nany Rubin and Julie Jaslow Auerbach

Oh,____ who are the peo- ple in my syn - a-gogue, in my syn a-gogue, in my syn - a - gogue. Oh, who are the peo- ple in my syn - agogue, the peo- ple that we meet each day?

1.Oh, the
2.Oh, the

Rab - bi leads us all in prayer.__ When we need the Rab - bi's al - ways
Can - tor sings our songs, you know,_____ Sing - ing high and sing - ing

THE PEOPLE IN OUR SYNAGOGUE

Words by Nany Rubin, Julie Jaslow Auerbach

REFRAIN: Oh, who are the people in my Synagogue,
In my Synagogue, in my Synagogue,
Oh, who are the people in my synagogue,
The people that we meet each day?

VERSES:

1.Oh, the Rabbi leads us all in prayer.
When we need, the Rabbi's always there.
We are visited when we're in school,
And we see the Rabbi in our shul.

    Refrain

2.Oh, the Cantor sings our songs, you know,
Singing high and singing low.
The Cantor shows us all the way,
Singing for us every day.

    Refrain

3.The Director of our school must run
A learning center that is fun.
Working hard, so when we're done
We'll show our stuff to everyone.

    Refrain

4.Oh, the Morah helps us all to learn
By letting each one take a turn
And tell of what we do each day.
Our teacher's loved in every way.

    Refrain

5.The Librarians lend out their books
For us to read, or just plain look.
Reading stories until we're hooked,
For Jews are "People of the Book."

LAST REFRAIN: Oh, the Rabbi is a person in my synagogue,
In my Synagogue, in my Synagogue.
And a Cantor is a person in my synagogue.
They're the people that you meet
When you come in from the street,
They're the people that you meet each day.

133. THE RABBI

Words by Jeffrey Klepper and Susan Nanus

Music by Jeffrey Klepper

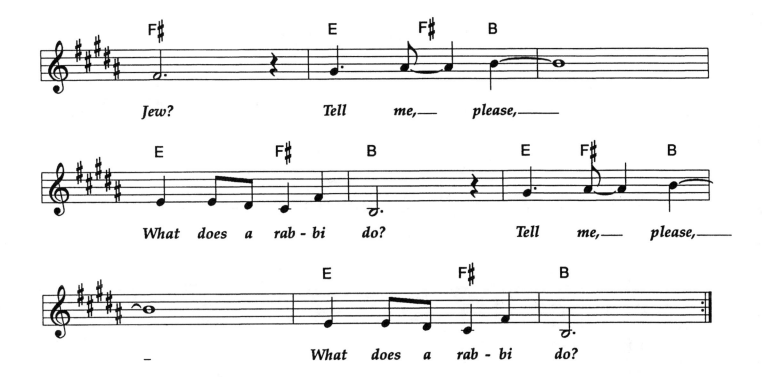

Jew? Tell me,— please,——

What does a rab - bi do? Tell me,— please,——

— What does a rab - bi do?

Verse 3
"Oh, people call me every day with problems big and small,
And though I wish I had more time, I try to help them all.
Then, of course, our lovely synagogue must be smoothly run.
That's some of the many things I do, and we've only just begun!"

    Refrain

Verse 4
"If helping the Jewish people is what you'd like to do,
Then to become a rabbi might be the thing for you.
So, if you work and study hard, a rabbi you might be,
That very special kind of Jew, just like you and me!"

    Refrain

134. THE CANTOR

Words and Music by Jeffrey Klepper

Verse 2
You can hear the cantor singing
With piano or guitar.
Jewish music is so special }
Because it tells us who we are. } (twice)

Refrain

Verse 3
So sing the songs of our people,
Sing along when you want to pray.
Sing when the cantor leads you,}
Sing at every holiday. } (twice)

Refrain

135. SAY THE B'RACHOT

Words and Music by Steven Carr Reuben

Verse 3

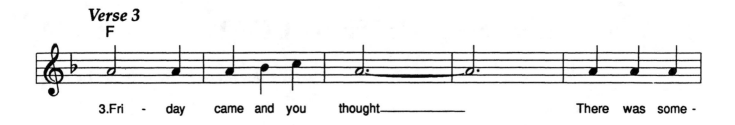

3.Fri - day came and you thought_____ There was some -

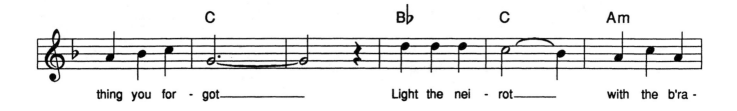

thing you for - got_____ Light the nei - rot_____ with the b'ra -

chot, say - ing, "L' - had - lik neir shel sha - bat."_____

136. PRAYER IS REACHING

Words and Music by Jeffrey Klepper

137. MODEH ANI

Morning Liturgy

Daniel Freelander and Jeffrey Klepper

I give thanks to you, O God, Eternal and living ruler, who in mercy, has returned my soul to me, great is your faithfulness.

מוֹדֶה אֲנִי לְפָנֶיךָ
מֶלֶךְ חַי וְקַיָּם.
שֶׁהֶחֱזַרְתָּ בִּי בְּנִשְׁמָתִי בְּחֶמְלָה
רַבָּה אֱמוּנָתֶךָ.

138. MAH TOVU
Round

Folk Song

How lovely are Your tents, O Jacob, your dwelling-places,
O Israel!

מַה־טֹּבוּ אֹהָלֶיךָ, יַעֲקֹב, מִשְׁכְּנֹתֶיךָ, יִשְׂרָאֵל!

139. YISM'CHU HASHAMAYIM

Liturgy   **Chassidic**

Let the heavens be glad and the earth rejoice. Let the sea
roar and all that fills it.

יִשְׂמְחוּ הַשָּׁמַיִם
וְתָגֵל הָאָרֶץ.
יִרְעַם הַיָּם וּמְלוֹאוֹ.

140. LA'ASOK B'DIVREI TORAH

Liturgy

Jeffrey Klepper

God commands us to engage
In the study of Torah

לַעֲסוֹק בְּדִבְרֵי תוֹרָה.

141. BAR'CHU

Ben Siegel

Arranged by Stephen Richards

Praise the One to whom our praise is due!
Praise the One to whom our praise is due,
Now and forever.

בָּרְכוּ אֶת־יְיָ הַמְבֹרָךְ!
בָּרוּךְ יְיָ הַמְבֹרָךְ לְעוֹלָם וָעֶד!

142. SH'MA YISRAEIL

Deuteronomy 6:4

Tzivika Pik

Hear, O Israel: the Eternal is our God, the Eternal is One!
Blessed is God's glorious kingdom for ever and ever!

שְׁמַע יִשְׂרָאֵל: יְיָ אֱלֹהֵינוּ יְיָ אֶחָד!
בָּרוּךְ שֵׁם כְּבוֹד מַלְכוּתוֹ לְעוֹלָם וָעֶד!

143. V'AHAVTA

Deuteronomy 6 **Michael Isaacson**

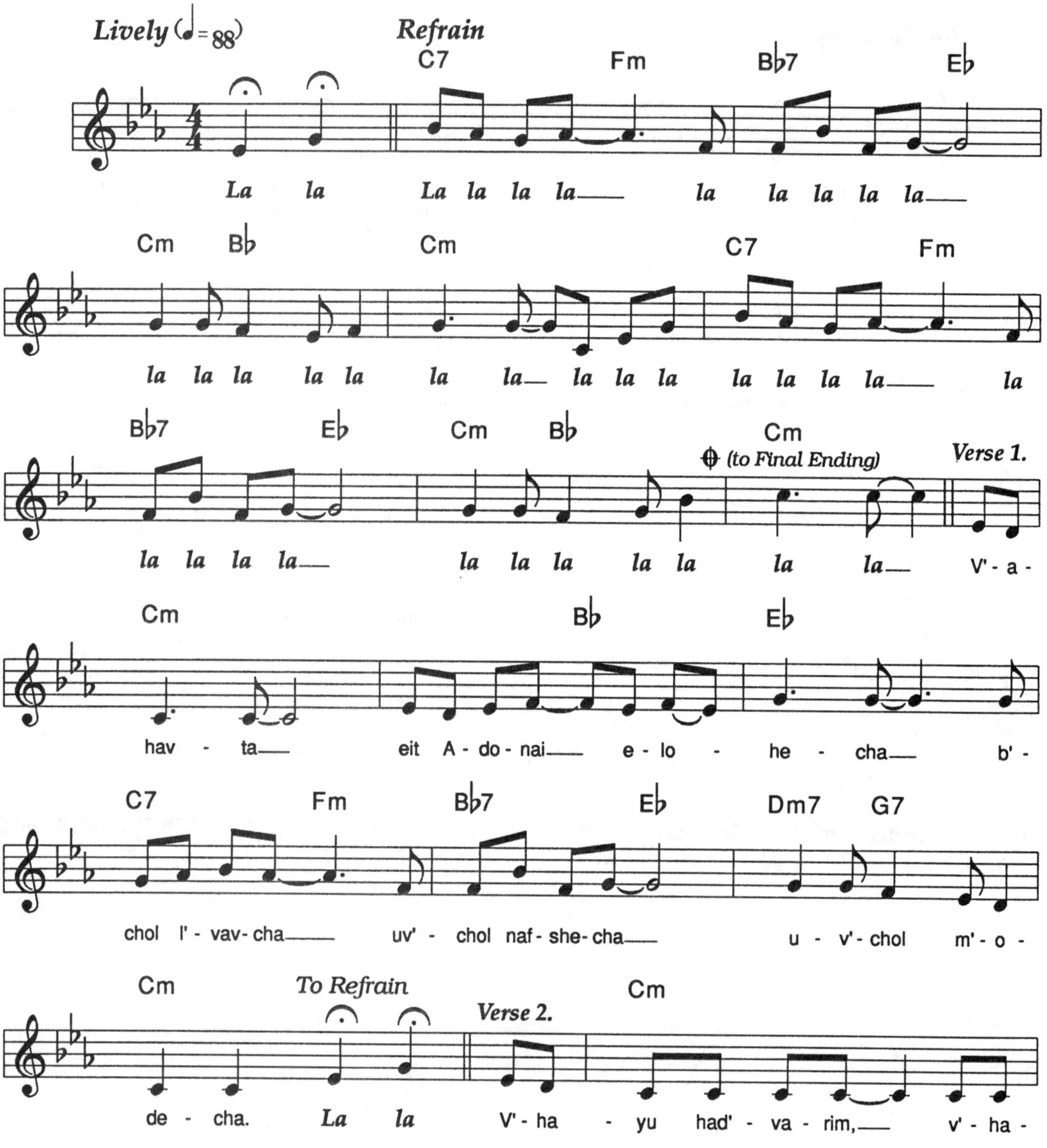

de - cha___ v'ha-yu l'-to-ta-fot bein ei-ne___-cha uch-
tav-tam___ al m'-zu-zot___ bei-te-cha,___ al m'-zu-zot___ bei-
te-cha___ u-vish-a-re___-cha.___ La la
La la___ la la la la la___ la la la la___ la la la la!

וְאָהַבְתָּ אֵת יְיָ אֱלֹהֶיךָ בְּכָל-לְבָבְךָ וּבְכָל-נַפְשְׁךָ וּבְכָל-מְאֹדֶךָ.
וְהָיוּ הַדְּבָרִים הָאֵלֶּה, אֲשֶׁר אָנֹכִי מְצַוְּךָ הַיּוֹם, עַל-לְבָבֶךָ.
וְשִׁנַּנְתָּם לְבָנֶיךָ, וְדִבַּרְתָּ בָּם בְּשִׁבְתְּךָ בְּבֵיתֶךָ, וּבְלֶכְתְּךָ
בַדֶּרֶךְ, וּבְשָׁכְבְּךָ וּבְקוּמֶךָ.

וּקְשַׁרְתָּם לְאוֹת עַל-יָדֶךָ, וְהָיוּ לְטֹטָפֹת בֵּין עֵינֶיךָ, וּכְתַבְתָּם
עַל-מְזֻזוֹת בֵּיתֶךָ, וּבִשְׁעָרֶיךָ.

You shall love the Lord your God with all your mind,
with all your strength, with all your being.
Set these words which I command you this day, upon
your heart. Teach them faithfully to your children; speak
of them in your home and on your way, when you lie
down and when you rise up.

Bind them as a sign upon your hand; let them be a
symbol before your eyes; inscribe them on the doorposts
of your house, and on your gates.

144. MI CHAMOCHA

Exodus 15   **Isadore Freed**

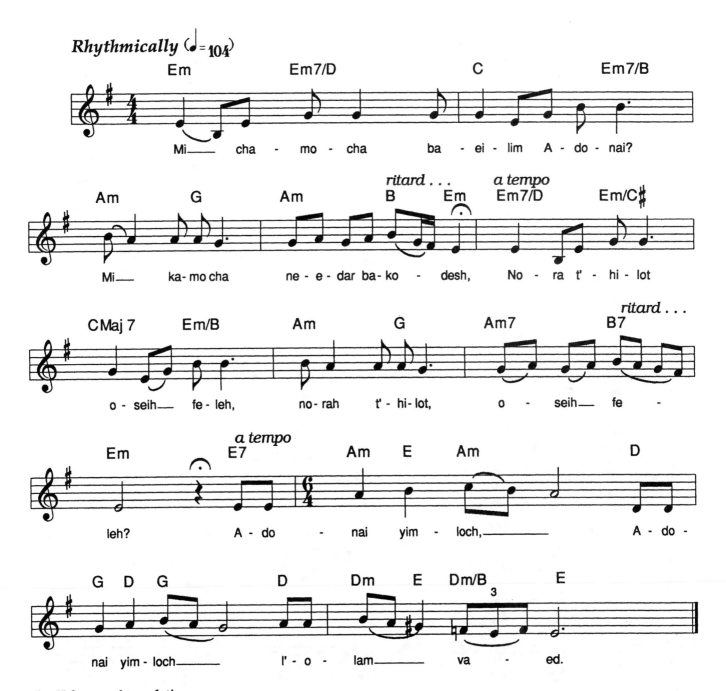

For Hebrew and translation
See number 58

145. OSEH SHALOM

Liturgy   **Nurit Hirsch**

For Hebrew and translation
See number 146

146. OSEH SHALOM

Liturgy   **Jeffrey Klepper**

May the One who causes peace to reign in the high
heavens,
let peace descend on us, on all Israel, and all the world,
and let us say: Amen.

עֹשֶׂה שָׁלוֹם בִּמְרוֹמָיו
הוּא יַעֲשֶׂה שָׁלוֹם עָלֵינוּ
וְעַל־כָּל־יִשְׂרָאֵל
וְאִמְרוּ אָמֵן.

147. OSEH SHALOM
Round

Liturgy

Debbie Friedman

For Hebrew and translation
See number 146

148. HODU LADONAI

Israel Alter

Arranged by Stephen Richards

O give thanks to the Lord, for He is good;
For God's love is everlasting.
Let Israel now say:
God's love is everlasting.
Let the House of Aaron now say:
God's love is everlasting.
Let all who revere the Lord now say:
God's love is everlasting.

הוֹדוּ לַיָי כִּי־טוֹב,
כִּי לְעוֹלָם חַסְדּוֹ.
יֹאמַר־נָא יִשְׂרָאֵל:
כִּי לְעוֹלָם חַסְדּוֹ.
יֹאמְרוּ־נָא בֵית־אַהֲרֹן:
כִּי לְעוֹלָם חַסְדּוֹ.
יֹאמְרוּ־נָא יִרְאֵי יְיָ:
כִּי לְעוֹלָם חַסְדּוֹ.

149. EIN KAMOCHA

Solomon Sulzer

There is none like You, Eternal One, among the gods,
and there are no deeds like Yours. You are with us to the
end of time; You are God through all generations.

You are with us always:
Eternal God, give strength to Your people;
Eternal God, bless Your people with peace.

אֵין כָּמוֹךָ בָאֱלֹהִים אֲדֹנָי וְאֵין כְּמַעֲשֶׂיךָ
מַלְכוּתְךָ מַלְכוּת כָּל-עֹלָמִים וּמֶמְשַׁלְתְּךָ בְּשָׁל-דּוֹר וָדוֹר.
יְהֹוָה מֶלֶךְ יְהֹוָה מָלָךְ יְהֹוָה יִמְלוֹךְ לְעוֹלָם וָעֶד.
יְהֹוָה עֹז לְעַמּוֹ יִתֵּן יְהֹוָה יְבָרֵךְ אֶת-עַמּוֹ בַשָּׁלוֹם.

150. TORAH SERVICE
Ki Mitzion; Baruch Shenatan

Solomon Sulzer

For out of Zion shall go forth Torah, and the word of God from Jerusalem.
We praise you: in holiness You give the Torah to Your people Israel.

כִּי מִצִּיּוֹן תֵּצֵא תוֹרָה וּדְבַר־יְיָ מִירוּשָׁלָיִם.
בָּרוּךְ שֶׁנָּתַן תּוֹרָה לְעַמּוֹ יִשְׂרָאֵל בִּקְדֻשָׁתוֹ.

151. TORAH SERVICE
Sh'ma; Echad Eloheinu; L'cha Adonai

Solomon Sulzer;
Gershon Ephros

שְׁמַע יִשְׂרָאֵל: יְיָ אֱלֹהֵינוּ יְיָ אֶחָד!

אֶחָד אֱלֹהֵינוּ גָּדוֹל אֲדוֹנֵינוּ קָדוֹשׁ שְׁמוֹ.

לְךָ יְיָ הַגְּדֻלָּה וְהַגְּבוּרָה וְהַתִּפְאֶרֶת וְהַנֵּצַח וְהַהוֹד

כִּי כֹל בַּשָּׁמַיִם וּבָאָרֶץ

לְךָ יְיָ הַמַּמְלָכָה וְהַמִּתְנַשֵּׂא לְכֹל לְרֹאשׁ.

Hear, O Israel: the Eternal is our God, the Eternal is One!
Our God is One; our God is great; holy is God's name.
In heaven, on earth, O God, are Your greatness, power,
glory, and beauty; for You are in all things. You are the
majestic, exalted God.

152. TORAH BLESSINGS
A. Before the Reading

Traditional

Freely

Bar' chu - et A-do nai ha-m'-vo rach, Ba - ruch A-do nai ha-m'-vo rach l'- o-lam va -

ed. Ba - ruch a - tah A - do - nai e - lo - hei - nu ma - lech ha - o -

lam a - sher ba - char ba-nu mi - kol ha - a - mim, v'- na - tan la-nu

et to - ra - to. Ba - ruch a - tah A - do - nai no - tein ha - to - rah.

בָּרְכוּ אֶת־יְיָ הַמְבֹרָךְ!

בָּרוּךְ יְיָ הַמְבֹרָךְ לְעוֹלָם וָעֶד!

בָּרוּךְ אַתָּה, יְיָ אֱלֹהֵינוּ, מֶלֶךְ הָעוֹלָם, אֲשֶׁר בָּחַר־בָּנוּ מִכָּל־
הָעַמִּים וְנָתַן־לָנוּ אֶת־תּוֹרָתוֹ. בָּרוּךְ אַתָּה, יְיָ, נוֹתֵן הַתּוֹרָה.

Praise the One to whom our praise is due!
Praised be the One to whom our praise is due, now and
for ever!
We praise you, God of time and space. You have called us
to serve You by giving us Your Torah. Praised be the
Eternal God, Giver of the Torah.

B. After the Reading

Freely

Ba — ruch a- tah A- do- nai e- lo -hei- nu me- lech ha- o - lam a- sher

na - tan la- nu to- rat e - met v'- cha- yei o- lam na- ta b'- to -

rit. . . .

chei- nu. Ba- ruch a - tah A- do- nai no- tein ha- to - rah.——

בָּרוּךְ אַתָּה, יְיָ אֱלֹהֵינוּ, מֶלֶךְ הָעוֹלָם, אֲשֶׁר נָתַן לָנוּ תּוֹרַת
אֱמֶת וְחַיֵּי עוֹלָם נָטַע בְּתוֹכֵנוּ. בָּרוּךְ אַתָּה, יְיָ, נוֹתֵן הַתּוֹרָה.

We praise You, God of time and space, who has given us a
Torah of truth, implanting within us eternal life. Praised
be the Eternal God, Giver of the Torah.

153. V'ZOT HATORAH

Avraham Tzvi Idelsohn

וְזֹאת הַתּוֹרָה אֲשֶׁר־שָׂם מֹשֶׁה לִפְנֵי בְּנֵי יִשְׂרָאֵל, עַל־פִּי יְיָ
בְּיַד־מֹשֶׁה.

This is the Torah that Moses placed before the people of
Israel to fulfill the word of God.

154. HODO AL ERETZ

Solomon Sulzer

Your splendor covers heaven and earth; You give strength to Your people; faithful Israel glories in You. Halleluyah!

הוֹדוֹ עַל אֶרֶץ וְשָׁמָיִם, וַיָּרֶם קֶרֶן לְעַמּוֹ, תְּהִלָּה לְכָל־חֲסִידָיו, לִבְנֵי יִשְׂרָאֵל עַם קְרוֹבוֹ. הַלְלוּיָהּ!

155. EITZ CHAYIM

Traditional

It is a tree of life to those who hold it fast, and all who cling to it find happiness. Its ways are ways of pleasantness, and all its paths are peace.

Help us to return to You, O God; then truly shall we return. Renew our days as in the past.

עֵץ-חַיִּים הִיא לַמַּחֲזִיקִים בָּהּ וְתֹמְכֶיהָ מְאֻשָּׁר.
דְּרָכֶיהָ דַרְכֵי-נֹעַם וְכָל-נְתִיבוֹתֶיהָ שָׁלוֹם.
הֲשִׁיבֵנוּ יְיָ אֵלֶיךָ וְנָשׁוּבָה.
חַדֵּשׁ יָמֵינוּ כְּקֶדֶם.

156. TREE OF LIFE
Round

Liturgy

Richard Silverman

For translation and Hebrew
See number 155

157. EILEH CHAMDAH LIBI

Round

Chassidic

This is my heart's desire: Be merciful and let us be close to You.

אֵלֶּה חָמְדָה לִבִּי
חוּסָה נָא וְאַל נָא תִּתְעַלֵּם.

158. EIN KEILOHEINU

Julius Freudenthal

אֵין כֵּאלֹהֵינוּ, אֵין כַּאדוֹנֵינוּ,
אֵין כְּמַלְכֵּנוּ, אֵין כְּמוֹשִׁיעֵנוּ.
מִי כֵאלֹהֵינוּ? מִי כַאדוֹנֵינוּ?
מִי כְמַלְכֵּנוּ? מִי כְמוֹשִׁיעֵנוּ?
נוֹדֶה לֵאלֹהֵינוּ, נוֹדֶה לַאדוֹנֵינוּ,
נוֹדֶה לְמַלְכֵּנוּ, נוֹדֶה לְמוֹשִׁיעֵנוּ.
בָּרוּךְ אֱלֹהֵינוּ, בָּרוּךְ אֲדוֹנֵינוּ,
בָּרוּךְ מַלְכֵּנוּ, בָּרוּךְ מוֹשִׁיעֵנוּ.
אַתָּה הוּא אֱלֹהֵינוּ,
אַתָּה הוּא אֲדוֹנֵינוּ,
אַתָּה הוּא מַלְכֵּנוּ,
אַתָּה הוּא מוֹשִׁיעֵנוּ.

There is none like our God, our Ruler and Redeemer
Who is like our God, our Ruler and Redeemer
We give thanks to our God, our Ruler and Redeemer
Praised be our God, our Ruler, our Redeemer
You alone are our God, our Ruler, our Redeemer

159. EIN ADIR

Sephardic Melody

אֵין אַדִּיר כַּיְיָ
וְאֵין בָּרוּךְ כְּבֶן עַמְרָם.
אֵין גְּדוֹלָה כַּתּוֹרָה
וְאֵין דַּרְשָׁנֶיהָ כְּיִשְׂרָאֵל.

מִפִּי אֵל וּמִפִּי אֵל
יְבֹרַךְ כָּל יִשְׂרָאֵל.

אֵין הָדוּר כַּיְיָ
וְאֵין וָתִיק כְּבֶן עַמְרָם.
אֵין זַכָּה כַּתּוֹרָה
וְאֵין חֲכָמֶיהָ כְּיִשְׂרָאֵל.

מִפִּי אֵל. . .

אֵין טָהוֹר כַּיְיָ
וְאֵין יָחִיד כְּבֶן עַמְרָם.
אֵין כַּבִּירָה כַּתּוֹרָה
וְאֵין לַמְדָנֶיהָ כְּיִשְׂרָאֵל.

מִפִּי אֵל. . .

אֵין פּוֹדֶה כַּיְיָ
וְאֵין צַדִּיק כְּבֶן עַמְרָם.
אֵין קְדוֹשָׁה כַּתּוֹרָה
וְאֵין תּוֹמְכֶיהָ כְּיִשְׂרָאֵל.

מִפִּי אֵל. . .

From the mouth of God,
let all Israel be blessed.

160. ADON OLAM

Liturgy

Uzi Hitman

- 237 -

אֲדוֹן עוֹלָם, אֲשֶׁר מָלַךְ
בְּטֶרֶם כָּל־יְצִיר נִבְרָא,
לְעֵת נַעֲשָׂה בְחֶפְצוֹ כֹּל,
אֲזַי מֶלֶךְ שְׁמוֹ נִקְרָא.
וְאַחֲרֵי כִּכְלוֹת הַכֹּל,
לְבַדּוֹ יִמְלוֹךְ נוֹרָא,
וְהוּא הָיָה, וְהוּא הֹוֶה,
וְהוּא יִהְיֶה בְּתִפְאָרָה.
וְהוּא אֶחָד, וְאֵין שֵׁנִי
לְהַמְשִׁיל לוֹ, לְהַחְבִּירָה,
בְּלִי רֵאשִׁית, בְּלִי תַכְלִית,
וְלוֹ הָעֹז וְהַמִּשְׂרָה.
וְהוּא אֵלִי, וְחַי גּוֹאֲלִי,
וְצוּר חֶבְלִי בְּעֵת צָרָה,
וְהוּא נִסִּי וּמָנוֹס לִי,
מְנָת כּוֹסִי בְּיוֹם אֶקְרָא.
בְּיָדוֹ אַפְקִיד רוּחִי
בְּעֵת אִישַׁן וְאָעִירָה,
וְעִם־רוּחִי גְּוִיָּתִי:
יְיָ לִי, וְלֹא אִירָא.

You are the Eternal God, who reigned before any being had been created; when all was done according to Your will, already then you were Sovereign. And after all has ceased to be, still will You reign in solitary majesty; You were, You are, You will be in glory. And you are One; none other can compare to You, or consort with You; You are without beginning, without end; Yours alone are power and dominion. And You are my God, my living Redeemer, my Rock in time of trouble and distress; You are my banner and my refuge, my benefactor when I call on you. Into Your hands I entrust my spirit, when I sleep and when I wake; my body also: You are with me, I shall not fear.

161. ADON OLAM

Eliezer Gerovitch

For translation and Hebrew
See number 160

162. ADON OLAM

French Sephardic Tune

For translation and Hebrew
See number 160

163. ADONAI OZ

Liturgy

Jeffrey Klepper

God, give strength to Your people.

יְיָ עֹז לְעַמּוֹ יִתֵּן יְיָ יְבָרֵךְ אֶת־עַמּוֹ בַשָּׁלוֹם.

164. V'NOMAR L'FANAV

Chassidic

We will sing unto God a new song!

וְנֹאמַר לְפָנָיו שִׁירָה חֲדָשָׁה, הַלְלוּיָהּ.

165. BIRKAT HAMAZON

Traditional tunes

Ra-bo-tai n'-va-reich. Y'—hi sheim A-do-nai m'-vo-rach mei-a-tah v'-ad o-

lam. Bir'—shut ma-ra-nan v'-ra-ba-nan v'-ra-bo-tai n'-va-

reich e-lo-hei-nu she-a-chal-nu mi-she-lo.

Ba—ruch e-lo-hei-nu she-a-chal-nu mi-she-lo___ uv'-tu-vo cha-yi-nu.

Ba-ruch hu u-va-ruch sh'-mo. Ba—ruch a-tah___ A-do-nai e-lo-

hei-nu me-lech ha-o-lam, ha—zan et ha-o-lam ku-lo b'-tu-vo b'-

chein v'—che-sed uv'-ra-cha-mim. Hu no-tein le-chem l'-chol ba-sar,

ki l'-o-lam chas-do. Uv'-tu-vo ha-ga-dol ta-mid al cha-sar la-nu

- 244 -

Leader:

רַבּוֹתַי נְבָרֵךְ.

Response:

יְהִי שֵׁם יְיָ מְבֹרָךְ מֵעַתָּה וְעַד עוֹלָם.

Leader:

בִּרְשׁוּת מָרָנָן וְרַבָּנָן וְרַבּוֹתַי, נְבָרֵךְ אֱלֹהֵינוּ שֶׁאָכַלְנוּ מִשֶּׁלוֹ.

Response:

בָּרוּךְ אֱלֹהֵינוּ שֶׁאָכַלְנוּ מִשֶּׁלוֹ וּבְטוּבוֹ חָיִינוּ.

Together:

בָּרוּךְ אַתָּה, יְיָ אֱלֹהֵינוּ, מֶלֶךְ הָעוֹלָם, הַזָּן אֶת הָעוֹלָם כֻּלוֹ
בְּטוּבוֹ. בְּחֵן, בְּחֶסֶד וּבְרַחֲמִים הוּא נוֹתֵן לֶחֶם לְכָל בָּשָׂר,
כִּי לְעוֹלָם חַסְדוֹ. וּבְטוּבוֹ הַגָּדוֹל תָּמִיד לֹא חָסַר לָנוּ, וְאַל
יֶחְסַר לָנוּ מָזוֹן לְעוֹלָם וָעֶד, בַּעֲבוּר שְׁמוֹ הַגָּדוֹל. כִּי הוּא
אֵל זָן וּמְפַרְנֵס לַכֹּל וּמֵטִיב לַכֹּל וּמֵכִין מָזוֹן לְכָל-בְּרִיוֹתָיו
אֲשֶׁר בָּרָא.

בָּרוּךְ אַתָּה, יְיָ, הַזָּן אֶת-הַכֹּל.

וּבְנֵה יְרוּשָׁלַיִם עִיר הַקֹּדֶשׁ בִּמְהֵרָה בְיָמֵינוּ. בָּרוּךְ אַתָּה,
יְיָ, בּוֹנֶה בְרַחֲמָיו יְרוּשָׁלָיִם. אָמֵן.

עֹשֶׂה שָׁלוֹם בִּמְרוֹמָיו, הוּא יַעֲשֶׂה שָׁלוֹם עָלֵינוּ וְעַל-כָּל-
יִשְׂרָאֵל, וְאִמְרוּ אָמֵן.

יְיָ עֹז לְעַמּוֹ יִתֵּן, יְיָ יְבָרֵךְ אֶת-עַמּוֹ בַשָּׁלוֹם.

Praised be the name of God, now and for ever!
Let us praise God.
Blessed is our God, of whose abundance we have eaten.
Blessed is our God, of whose abundance we have eaten,
and by whose goodness we live.
Blessed is the One-Who-Is!
Blessed is the Eternal our God, Ruler of the universe,
whose goodness sustains the world. The God of grace,
love, and compassion is the Source of food for all who
live – for God's love is everlasting. Through God's great
goodness we do not lack and will never lack. For God is
in the goodness that sustains and nourishes all,
providing food enough for every living being.
Blessed is the Eternal Source of food for all who live.
O let Jerusalem, the holy city, be renewed in our time.
Blessed is the Eternal by whose compassion we will see
Jerusalem renewed and at peace. Amen.
May the One who causes peace to reign in the High
Heavens, let peace descend on us, on all of Israel, and on
all the world and let us say: Amen.
Eternal God bless your people with peace.

166. THE TORAH

Words by Jeffrey Klepper and Susan Nanus   **Music by Jeffrey Klepper**

For Hebrew and translation
See number 155

167. B'REISHIT 1: 1-5

Torah Chant

Very free tempo

or_____ u-vein ha - cho-shech. 5.Va-yik - ra E-lo-him_____ la-or,

yom_____ v'-la - cho - shech_ ka-ra_____ lai-lah; va-y'-hi

e - rev, va-y'-hi vo - ker, yom e - chad._____

בְּרֵאשִׁית בָּרָא אֱלֹהִים אֵת הַשָּׁמַיִם וְאֵת הָאָרֶץ:
וְהָאָרֶץ הָיְתָה תֹהוּ וָבֹהוּ וְחֹשֶׁךְ עַל-פְּנֵי תְהוֹם
וְרוּחַ אֱלֹהִים מְרַחֶפֶת עַל-פְּנֵי הַמָּיִם:
וַיֹּאמֶר אֱלֹהִים יְהִי-אוֹר וַיְהִי-אוֹר:
וַיַּרְא אֱלֹהִים אֶת-הָאוֹר כִּי-טוֹב
וַיַּבְדֵּל אֱלֹהִים בֵּין הָאוֹר וּבֵין הַחֹשֶׁךְ:
וַיִּקְרָא אֱלֹהִים לָאוֹר יוֹם וְלַחֹשֶׁךְ קָרָא לָיְלָה
וַיְהִי-עֶרֶב וַיְהִי-בֹקֶר יוֹם אֶחָד.

In the beginning God created the heavens and the earth. And the earth was without form and void, and there was darkness upon the face of the deep, and the spirit of God moved over the surface of the waters. Then God said: Let there be light! and there was light. God saw that the light was good, and God separated the light from the darkness. God called the light Day, and the darkness Night. And there was evening and there was morning , one day.

168. THIS IS VERY GOOD
(When God Made The World)

Words By Chaim Stern   **Music by Jeffrey Klepper**

© Copyright 1991 by Jeffrey Klepper

169. RISE AND SHINE

Folk Song

Lively (♩=120)

Verses

The Lord said to No- ah, there's gon- na be a flood- y, flood- y!

Lord said to No- ah, there's gon na be a flood- y, flood- y! Get those child- ren

out of the mud- y, mud- dy, child- ren___ of the Lord.___ So,

Refrain

rise___ and shine___ and give God your glo- ry, glo- ry!

Rise___ and shine___ and give God your glo- ry, glo- ry! Rise and shine and

give God your glo- ry, glo- ry! Child- ren___ of the Lord!___

Verse 1
The Lord said to Noah, there's gonna be a floody, floody!
Lord said to Noah, there's gonna be a floody, floody!
Get those children out of the muddy, muddy,
Children of the Lord.

Refrain:

So, rise and shine and give God your glory, glory!
 Rise and shine and give God your glory, glory!
Rise and shine and give God your glory, glory!
Children of the Lord!

Verse 2
So Noah he built them, he built them an arky, arky! (twice)
Made it out of hick'ry barky barky!
Children of the Lord.

Refrain

Verse 3
The animals, they came on, they came on by twosies, twosies (twice)
Elephants and kkangaroosies - roosies!
Children of the Lord.

Refrain

Verse 4
 It rained and poured for forty daysies, daysies (twice)
Drove those animals nearly crazy, crazy!
Children of the Lord.

Refrain

Verse 5
The sun came out and dried up the landy, landy (twice)
Everything was fine and dandy, dandy!
Children of the Lord.

Refrain

170. NOAH AND THE ARK

Words by Joel Funk and Dan Funk

Music by Joel Funk

Folk style (♩=96)

It hap-pened ma-ny years a-go___ the Bi - ble tells___ the tale. The

world was full of e - vil men so No - ah had___ to set sail.___

___ He heard a voice___ in his sleep one night the

Lord said: "Noah, get out of sight.___ There's gon - na be___ a lot of rain.___ I

want to start a - gain."___

1.So No - ah built him an
2.The sky grew cloud - y, and

ark made___ out of wood. The Lord had spared him be cause___ he was
day turned___ in - to night. Thun - der and light - ning brought pa - nic and___

F7

good._____ Then No - ah gath-ered all his clan,___ his
fright._____ Too late the wick - ed kneeled to pray._____

Eb **F** **Bb**

Eb **F** **Bb**   **Eb** **F** **Bb**

wife and sons,__ Ja- peth Shem and Ham.__ The Lord said: "No - ah, just one thing,__
All the e - vil was washed a - way.__ The rain came down for for - ty days and

Eb **D7** **Gm** **D7**   **Eb** **F** **Bb**

Here's the crea - tures you shall bring. Go gath - er two____ of ev' - ry kind,
for - ty___ nights.____ The ark went on___ a whirl - pool ride.

Gm **C7** **F7**   **Eb** **F** **Bb**

All the oth - ers shall stay be - hind__ Se-ven pairs__ of fly - ing birds and
All the peo - ple were safe in - side.__ For-ty days__ had passed at last and

Gm **Cm** **F**   **F**

ko - sher things._____ He round - ed all__ the crea - tures up__ and
none too fast._____ They land - ed on__ a mount - ain top__ and

Bb   **F**

led them in - to the boat. The peo - ple snick - ered and they laughed,__ "On
called it A - ra-rat peak, He sent a dove__ who soon re - turned,__ an

Bb   **F** **Eb** **F**

land it's not__ gon-na float!" But No - ah warned,__ "You'll change your tune,__ for
ol - ive branch__ in its beak. The ol - ive branch__ meant there would be__ a

171. KESHET
(Rainbow)

Judy Caplan Ginsburgh

Simply (♩ = 116)

Ke - shet, ke - shet, I like to see you up in the sky so
(Rain - bow, rain - bow,)

pret - ty. You hide your face 'til af - ter it rains,

Then paint the sky with your col - ors. Ke - shet, ke - shet,
(Rain - bow, rain - bow,)

pur - ple and pink, red yel - low blue and o - range. Ke - shet, ke - shet,
(Rain - bow, rain - bow,)

I'd like to see you up in the sky more of - ten.

172. UFARATZTA

Genesis 28:14

Chassidic

You shall spread out to the west and to the east, to the north and to the south. All the families of the earth shall bless themselves by you and your descendants.

וּפָרַצְתָּ יָמָה וָקֵדְמָה
וְצָפֹנָה וָנֶגְבָּה
וְנִבְרְכוּ בְךָ
כָּל־מִשְׁפְּחֹת
הָאֲדָמָה וּבְזַרְעֶךָ

173. ERETZ ZAVAT CHALAV
(Round)

Deuteronomy 27:3

Emanuel Gamliel

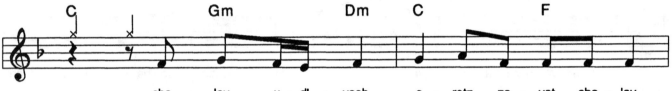

A land flowing with milk and honey.

אֶרֶץ זָבַת חָלָב וּדְבַשׁ

174. MI CHAMOCHA
Chant from "Song of the Sea"

Exodus 15: 11, 18   **Shirat Hayam Chant**

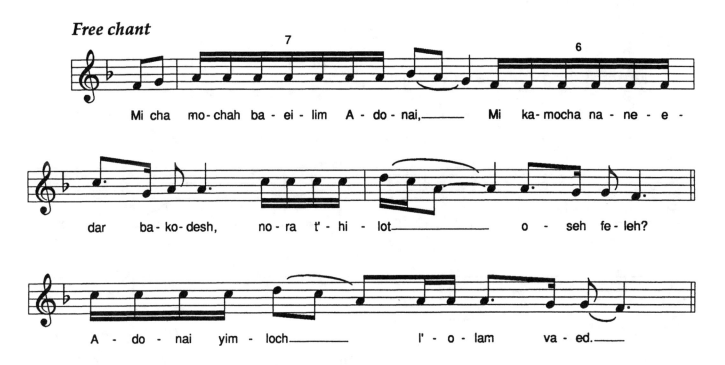

Free chant

Mi cha mo-chah ba-ei-lim A-do-nai,_____ Mi ka-mocha na-ne-e-

dar ba-ko-desh, no-ra t'-hi-lot_____ o - seh fe-leh?

A - do - nai yim - loch_____ l' - o - lam va - ed._____

For translation and Hebrew
See number 58

175. TEN COMMANDMENTS

Words by Jeffrey Klepper and Jeffrey Salkin

Music by Jeffrey Klepper

murder another is a terrible wrong;___ (7)A
marriage must be built on trust; (8)Never steal, be honest and
just. (9)Don't lie when you're on the witness stand; (10)Do
not desire___ what your neighbor has.___ Follow these laws that

D.C. al Fine

I will give, for they will help___ you live.

176. V'AHAVTA

Deuteronomy 6

Torah Chant

For translation and Hebrew
See number 143

177. BUILDING SOLOMON'S TEMPLE

Lucille Gechtman
after "Old MacDonald"
Arranged by Stephen Richards

King Sol-o-mon built the Ho - ly Tem-ple man - y years a -

go.   And   all   day   long   his   peo-ple   were   bu - sy

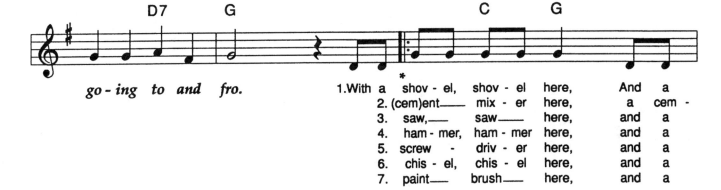

go - ing   to   and   fro.

1. With a shov - el, shov - el here,   And a
2. (cem)ent___ mix - er here,   a cem -
3. saw,___ saw___ here,   and a
4. ham - mer, ham - mer here,   and a
5. screw - driv - er here,   and a
6. chis - el, chis - el here,   and a
7. paint___ brush___ here,   and a

shov - el, shov - el there.	Here a shov - el, there a shov - el,
ent___ mix - er there.	Here a mix - er, there a mix - er,
saw,___ saw___ there.	Here a saw,___ there a saw,___
ham - mer, ham - mer there.	Here a ham - mer, there a ham - mer,
screw - driv - er there.	Here a driv - er, there a driv - er,
chis - el, chis - el there.	Here a chis - el, there a chis - el,
paint___ brush___ there.	Here a brush,___ there a brush,___

ev - 'ry - where a shov - el, shov - el. · *Sol-o mon built the Ho - ly Tem-ple*
ev - 'ry - where a cem - ent mix - er.
ev - 'ry - where a saw,____ saw.____
ev - 'ry - where a ham - mer, ham - mer.
ev - 'ry - where a screw____ driv - er.
ev - 'ry - where a chis - el, chis - el.
ev - 'ry - where a paint____ brush.____

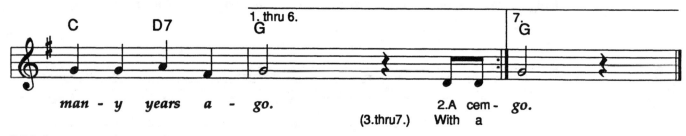

man - y years a - go.   *2.A cem - go.*
          (3.thru7.)   *With a*

*Make appropriate action

178. DAVID MELECH YISRAEIL

Folk Song

David, king of Israel, lives and endures.

דָּוִד מֶלֶךְ יִשְׂרָאֵל
חַי וְקַיָּם.

179. ISAIAH 42: 5,6

Haftarah Chant

Freely; Note values are approximate

Koh a -mar_____ ha - eil_____ A - do - nai_____ bo -

rei___ ha - sha - ma - yim v' - no - tei - hem,___ ro - ka___ ha - a - retz v' - tze - e - tza -

e - ha; no - tein___ n' - sha - mah___ la - am___ a - le - ha, v' - ru - ach la -

hol - chim bah.___ A - ni_____ A - do - nai_____ k' - ra -

ti - cha v' - tze - dek v' - ach - zeik b' - ya - de - cha; v' - e - tzar -

cha,_____ v' - e - ten - cha,___ liv - rit___ am___ l' - or go - yim.___

כֹּה־אָמַר הָאֵל יְהֹוָה
בּוֹרֵא הַשָּׁמַיִם וְנוֹטֵיהֶם
רֹקַע הָאָרֶץ וְצֶאֱצָאֶיהָ
נֹתֵן נְשָׁמָה לָעָם עָלֶיהָ
וְרוּחַ לַהֹלְכִים בָּהּ׃
אֲנִי יְהֹוָה קְרָאתִיךָ בְצֶדֶק
וְאַחֲזֵק בְּיָדֶךָ
וְאֶצָּרְךָ וְאֶתֶּנְךָ
לִבְרִית עָם לְאוֹר גּוֹיִם׃

Thus said God,
Who created the heavens and stretched them out,
Who spread out the earth and what it brings forth,
Who gave breath to the people upon it
And life to those who work thereon:
I the Eternal, in My grace, have called you,
And I have grasped you by the hand.
I created you, and appointed you
A covenant people, a light unto the nations

180. LO YISA GOI

Isaiah 2:4

Shalom Altman

Nation shall not lift up sword against nation, nor ever
again shall they train for war.

לֹא יִשָּׂא גוֹי אֶל גּוֹי חֶרֶב,
לֹא יִלְמְדוּ עוֹד מִלְחָמָה.

181. DODI LI

Song of Songs 2:16, 3:6, 4:9

Steven Sher

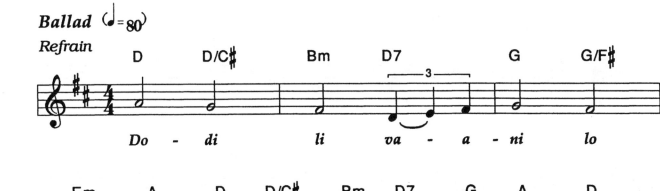

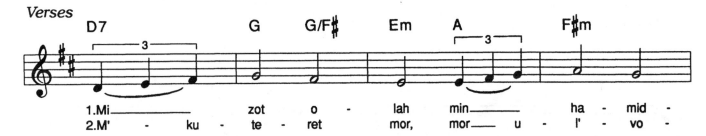

My beloved is mine and I am his, who feeds among the lilies.
Who is this coming up from the desert, burning myrrh and frankincense?
You have ravished my heart my sister, my bride.
Awake, O North wind, come, O South wind.

דוֹדִי לִי וַאֲנִי לוֹ הָרוֹעֶה בַּשׁוֹשַׁנִּים.
מִי זֹאת עֹלָה מִן הַמִּדְבָּר
מְקֻטֶּרֶת מֹר וּלְבוֹנָה.
לִבַּבְתִּנִי אֲחוֹתִי כַלָּה.
עוּרִי צָפוֹן וּבוֹאִי תֵימָן.

182. KUMI LACH

Song of Songs 2:10-11

Debbie Friedman

Rise, my love, my beauty, come away.
For lo the winter is over,
The rain is past and gone.

קוּמִי לָךְ רַעְיָתִי יָפָתִי קוּמִי לָךְ
כִּי הִנֵּה הַסְּתָו עָבָר
הַגֶּשֶׁם חָלַף הָלַךְ לוֹ.

183. HAL'LUYAH; HINEIH MAH TOV
Round

Psalms 133: 1   **Ecumenical Youth Service**

How good it is, and how pleasant,
when brothers and sisters dwell together in unity.

הִנֵּה מַה־טּוֹב וּמַה־נָּעִים
שֶׁבֶת אַחִים גַּם־יָחַד.

184. HOW GLORIOUS

Based on Psalm 8

Word and Music by Les Bronstein

- 275 -

185. AL TIFG'I VI

Ruth I: 16-17

Lawrence Avery

Al tif-g'i vi l'-oz-veich la-shuv, la - shuv mei-a-cha-ra - yich. Ki el a-sher teil-chi ei - leich u-va-a-sher ta-li-ni a -lin; A - meich a - mi vei-lo- ha - yich e-lo - hai. A - meich a - mi vei-lo- ha-yich e-lo - hai. Ba-a-sher ta - mu-ti a-

mut v'-sham, v'-sham ___ e-ka-veir; ___ Koh ya-a-

seh A-do-nai li, v'-choh yo-sif, v'-choh ___ yo-sif.

Ki ha-ma-vet yaf-rid bei-

ni ___ u-vei-neich. ___

"Do not urge me to leave you, to turn back and not
follow you. For wherever you go, I will go; wherever you
lodge, I will lodge; your people shall be my people, and
your God my God. Where you die, I will die, and there I
will be buried. Thus and more may do to me if anything
but death parts me from you."

אַל תִּפְגְּעִי בִי לְעָזְבֵךְ
לָשׁוּב מֵאַחֲרָיִךְ
כִּי אֶל אֲשֶׁר תֵּלְכִי אֵלֵךְ
וּבַאֲשֶׁר תָּלִינִי אָלִין
עַמֵּךְ עַמִּי וֵאלֹהַיִךְ אֱלֹהָי.
בַּאֲשֶׁר תָּמוּתִי אָמוּת וְשָׁם אֶקָּבֵר.
כֹּה יַעֲשֶׂה יְיָ וְכֹה יוֹסִיף
כִּי הַמָּוֶת יַפְרִיד בֵּינִי וּבֵינֵךְ.

186. AL SH'LOSHAH D'VARIM

Pirkei Avot 1:2

Chaim Zur

The world depends on three things: on Torah, on
worship, and on acts of loving kindness.

עַל־שְׁלשָׁה דְבָרִים
הָעוֹלָם עוֹמֵד:
עַל הַתּוֹרָה,
וְעַל הָעֲבוֹדָה,
וְעַל גְּמִילוּת חֲסָדִים.

187. AMAR RABI AKIVA

Sifra: K'doshim

Folk Melody

Said Rabbi Akiva: "You shall love your neighbor as yourself" – this is the great principle of the Torah.

אָמַר רַבִּי עֲקִיבָא
וְאָהַבְתָּ לְרֵעֲךָ כָּמוֹךָ:
זֶה כְּלָל גָּדוֹל בַּתּוֹרָה.

188. AMAR RABI ELAZAR

Talmud: Berakot 64A

Folk Melody

Rabbi Elazar said, quoting Rabbi Chanina: "The disciples of the wise (students of Torah) add peace to the world."

אָמַר רַבִּי אֶלְעָזָר,
אָמַר רַבִּי חֲנִינָא:
תַּלְמִידֵי חֲכָמִים
מַרְבִּים שָׁלוֹם בָּעוֹלָם.

189. LO ALECHA

Pirkei Avot 2:21

Daniel Freelander and Jeffrey Klepper

It is not your duty to complete the work.
But neither are you free to desist from it.

לֹא עָלֶיךָ הַמְּלָאכָה לִגְמוֹר
וְלֹא אַתָּה בֶּן חוֹרִין לְהִבָּטֵל מִמֶּנָּה

190. IM EIN ANI LI

Pirkei Avot 1:14; Haggadah liturgy

Debbie Friedman

If I am not for myself, who will be for me? But if I am for myself alone, what am I? And if not now, when?

אִם אֵין אֲנִי לִי מִי לִי?
וּכְשֶׁאֲנִי לְעַצְמִי
מָה אֲנִי?
וְאִם לֹא עַכְשָׁו אֵימָתַי,
אֵימָתַי?

191. WHAT IS A MITZVAH?

Words and Music by Barbara Bar-Nissim

Bouncy (♩ = 120)

What is a Mitz - vah?___ We want to know!___

It's a good deed___ that makes good feel-ings grow.___ Why should we do___ them?___

We want to know.___ For our- selves and for God,___ to make good feel-ings grow.___ *Fine*

Verses

1. Vis - it your grand - pa___ when he is sick___ a
2. Hon - or your par - ents,___ Be kind to your pet.___ Be

mitz - vah like that___ might get him well quick.___ Call up your grand - ma___ and
nice to your friends, Show your teach - er res - pect.___ Be sure to light can - dles___ on

D.C. al Fine

just say, "Hel-lo."___ May - be help your par - ents when they're shov - el - ing snow.___
Er - ev Shab-bat;___ say "Kid - dush" and "Mo - tzi" and Mitz - vahs you've got!___

192. GIVING

Words and Music by Fran Avni

With feeling (♩ = 116)

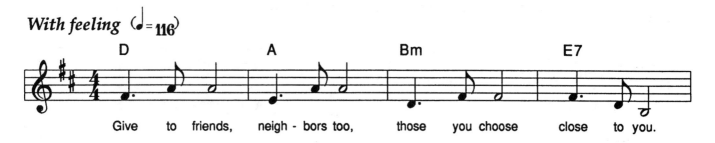

Give to friends, neigh - bors too, those you choose close to you.

Give your time, spare a dime, a - ny thing will do.

There's no "Yours" or "Mine" in shar - ing._____ Giv - ing

makes you feel so lov - ing,___ does - n't it? Lov - ing_____

ritard . . .

___ makes you feel like giv - ing at least a lit - tle bit, does - n't it?

a tempo

Give to friends, stran-gers, too, those who're not as luck-y as you.

Give your time, spare a dime, a-ny thing will do.

There's no "Yours" or "Mine" in shar-ing.

Coda

There's no "Yours" or "Mine," There's no "Yours" or "Mine,"

There's no "Yours" or "Mine" in shar-ing.

193. HEROES

Words and Music by Bruce Benson

REFRAIN: **We won't let go,**
We won't let go,
We won't let go 'til Pharoah sets them free!

1. There are some that we helped bring to freedom,
And for that alone we can be proud,
But still it is our future obligation
To stand firm and sing out loud:

    REFRAIN

2. We stand in defiance of the wicked,
We stand while our brothers are enslaved,
But if there is just one voice left behind the iron wall,
Then freedom is distant still for all.

3. There's only one way for the righteous,
There's only one way for the true,
To fight for the rights of the many.
We know they'll all be free before we're through.

    REFRAIN

4. There are some that we helped bring to freedom,
And for that alone we can stand tall,
But still it is our future obligation,
To stand firm until we've freed them all.

5. We sing the songs of our heroes,
We sing the songs that set them free,
We sing the songs we sing to let the wicked know:

    REFRAIN

194. EILI, EILI

Hannah Szenesh

David Zahavi

O God, my God,
I pray that these things never end:
The sand and the sea,
The rush of the waters,
The crash of the heavens,
The prayer of the heart.

אֵלִי אֵלִי

שֶׁלֹּא יִגָּמֵר לְעוֹלָם

הַחוֹל וְהַיָּם

רִשְׁרוּשׁ שֶׁל הַמַּיִם

בְּרַק הַשָּׁמַיִם

תְּפִלַּת הָאָדָם.

195. ANI V'ATAH

Arik Einstein   **Miki Gabriellov**

1. You and I will change the world – then everyone
   will join us.
   It's been said before, but it doesn't matter.
   You and I will change the world.

2. You and I will try to start from the beginning.
   It'll be tough but so what, it doesn't matter.
   You and I will change the world.

אֲנִי וְאַתָּה נְשַׁנֶּה אֶת הָעוֹלָם,

אֲנִי וְאַתָּה אָז יָבוֹאוּ כְּבָר כֻּלָּם,

אָמְרוּ אֶת זֶה קֹדֶם לְפָנַי

לֹא מְשַׁנֶּה – אֲנִי וְאַתָּה נְשַׁנֶּה אֶת הָעוֹלָם.

אֲנִי וְאַתָּה נְנַסֶּה מֵהַתְחָלָה,

יִהְיֶה לָנוּ רַע, אֵין דָּבָר זֶה לֹא נוֹרָא,

אָמְרוּ אֶת זֶה קֹדֶם לְפָנַי,

זֶה לֹא מְשַׁנֶּה – אֲנִי וְאַתָּה נְשַׁנֶּה אֶת הָעוֹלָם.

196. LET THE HEAVENS BE GLAD

Psalms 99:11, 133:1
Leviticus 25:10
Joel 3:1

Robert Weinberg

Joyfully (♩ = 168)

Refrain
Let the heav - ens— be glad, let— the heav - ens be—
glad, let the earth re - joice,— let the sea roar,— let

1. peo - ple— u - nite.
2. Let the peo - ple— u - nite.

to coda
to verses

1. Be - hold how good and— how pleas - ant it is— for
peo - ple to live in— peace.— Be - hold how good it is,—
peo - ple———— live in— peace!————— Let the

to Refrain

197. YAD B'YAD
Hand in Hand

Words and Music by Craig Taubman

Yad b'-yad___ e-chad im ha-shei-ni

Am e-chad___ im leiv e-chad___ kein a-nu nad-lik, nad-

lik m'-su-at___ o-lam___ nad-li-ka ka-am___ e-chad.

Yad b'-yad___ e-chad, e-chad___ kein a-nu nad-lik.

Round

יָד בְּיָד אֶחָד עִם הַשֵּׁנִי
עַם אֶחָד עִם לֵב אֶחָד
כֵּן אָנוּ נַדְלִיק
נַדְלִיק מַשּׂוּאֹת עוֹלָם
נַדְלִיק כְּעַם אֶחָד
יָד בְּיָד אֶחָד אֶחָד
כֵּן אָנוּ נַדְלִיק
אִם אֵין קֶמַח אֵין תּוֹרָה
אִם אֵין תּוֹרָה אֵין קֶמַח.

It can be you, it can be me.
It can be people all over the world
Lending, caring, sharing hand in hand.

- 296 -

198. OT PUSTYI NAROD MOI
(Let My People Go!)

Song of the Russian Jews

* Rhymes with "boy."

199. LEAVING MOTHER RUSSIA

Words and Music by Robert Solomon

wait - ed___ far too long, We are leav - ing___ Moth - er Rus-

sia,___ When they come for us___ we'll be gone.

Final ending

come for us we'll be gone, we'll be gone.___

2. For all those centuries we called this land our home,
We loved the Russian soil as much as anyone.
In countless armies our young boys have died for you
But never did you call them "sons," you always called them, "Jew!"
We fell in battle for the Tsar; A hundred thousand died at Babi Yar,
And yet your monument denies their faith, while on our passport we read: "yevrai."

Refrain

3. I send my song of hope to those I left behind,
I pray that they may know the freedom that is mine,
For in my darkest hour alone inside my cell I kept the vision of my home in Yisraeil.
My friend, we know what silence brings; another Hitler waiting in the wings.
So stand up now and shout it to the sky,
Though they bring us to our knees we will never die!

Refrain

200. THE RAINBOW COVENANT

Words and Music by Robert Solomon

1.As I went walk - ing one ear - ly morn

I passed the gar - den where I was born

And all a - round me Spread high and wide_____ A wall of

col - ors Reached to the sky._____

Rain - bow,— rain - bow, rain-bow, rain - bow._____

Rain - bow,— rain - bow, rain-bow, rain - bow._____

2.And— the
3.And— the

Lord said to No - ah:_____ Here is My sign— to you, it is a
Lord said to No - ah:_____ This is My gift— to you, it is a

201. JUST ANOTHER FOREIGNER

Words by
Robert Solomon and Joel Sussman

Music by Joel Sussman

Sit-ting in a hall in Ki - ri - at Sh'mo-neh___ with Jews from Sy - ri - a, from Ye - men and I - ran, The on - ly Ash - ke - na - zi in Ki - ri - at Sh'mo-neh.___ I can hear their laugh - ter but I can - not un - der - stand.___ Just a - noth - er for - eign - er in a - noth - er for - eign land, but these strang-ers are my broth-ers as they take me by the hand, sing - ing: "A - lei-kem sa-laam, Sha - lom a - lei - chem!" Heim sha - ru: "B'ru - chim ha-ba-im, sha - lom a - lei - chem!"

Verse 1
Sitting in a hall in Kiryat Sh'moneh.
With Jews from Syria,
            from Yemen and Iran,
The only Ashkenazi in Kiryat Sh'moneh.
I can hear their laughter
            but I cannot understand.

Chorus
Just another foreigner
            in another foreign land,
But these strangers are my brothers
            as they take me by the hand.
"Aleikhem salaam, Salaam aleikhem,
B'ruchim haba'im, shalom aleichem."

Verse 2
I met a man from Addis Ababa,
His skin was black
            and his features kind of strange.
He showed me a book
            that he said was the Torah,
And spoke of his people,
            and Falasha was their name.

Chorus
Just another foreigner
            in another foreign land,
But I knew he was my brother
            when he took me by the hand.
"Oh, Tanasteling, shalom aleichem,
B'ruchim haba'im, shalom aleichem."

Verse 3
A woman returns
            on the streets of Odessa,
From looking for a job
            in the cold Russian wind.
It's been five hungry years
            while she waits for a visa.
She still lights the candles
            as Shabbos begins.

Chorus
Just another foreigner
            in another foreign land,
But she's joining all her people
            as she follows God's command.
"Oh, Zhdarovah, shalom aleichem,
B'ruchim haba'im, shalom aleichem."

Welcome my brothers, welcome one and all!
Welcome my sisters, welcome one and all!
B'ruchim haba'im, shalom aleichem!

INDEX BY TITLE

Title	Last Name	First Name	Page	Pre-Sch	Primary	Intermediate
Hatikvah	Folk Themes		184		PR	IN
Havah Nagilah	Idelsohn	A.Z.	16	ps	PR	IN
Hayom Yom Huledet	Richards	Stephen	45	ps		
Heiveinu Shalom Aleichem	Folk Song			ps	PR	IN
Heroes	Benson	Bruce	287		PR	IN
Hey-Man!	Richards	Stephen	126		PR	
Hineh Ma Tov	Folk Song		8	ps	PR	
Hodo Al Eretz	Sulzer	Solomon	228			IN
Hodu Ladonai	Alter	Israel	219			IN
How Glorious	Bronstein	Les	273			IN
I Am the Afikomen	Friedman	Debbie	136	ps	PR	IN
I'm Growing	Klepper	Jeffrey	28	ps	PR	
I'm Proud To Be A Jew	Reuben	Steven Carr	38		PR	
If I Were a Candle	Serling	Elaine	106	ps	PR	IN
Im Ein Ani Li	Friedman	Debbie	282		PR	IN
Im Tirzu	Friedman	Debbie	177		PR	IN
Isaiah 42:5,6	Haftarah Chant		266			IN
Jewish Calendar Song	Auerbach	Julie Jaslow	60		PR	
Jewish Life Cycle Song	Auerbach	Julie Jaslow	40		PR	
Just Another Foreigner	Sussman	Joel	301			IN
K'chol V'lavan	Folk Song-Russian		178	ps	PR	IN
Kadeish Urchatz	Folk Song-Babylonian		148			IN
Kareiv Yom	Folk Song		139			IN
Keshet-Rainbow	Ginsburgh	Judy Caplan	256	ps	PR	
Ki Eshm'ra Shabbat	Folk Song-Baghdad		84		PR	IN
Kiddush-Erev Shabbat	Lewandoski	Louis	79			IN
Kippah	Klepper	Jeffrey	191	ps	PR	
Kol Nidre	Traditional Nusach		95			IN
Kum Bachur Atzeil	Folk Song		172	ps	PR	IN
Kumi Lach	Friedman	Debbie	270			IN
L'chah Dodi	Folk Song		70		PR	IN
	Zeira	Mordechai	72			IN
L'Shanah Tovah	Traditional Tune		89	ps	PR	
Laasok B'divrei Torah	Klepper	Jeffrey	208		PR	IN
Lach Y'rushalayim	Rubenstein	Eli	182			IN
Last Butterfly	Shenson	Lisa Glatzer	164		PR	IN
Leaving Mother Russia	Solomon	Robert	297			IN
Let the Heavens Be Glad	Weinberg	Robert	291			IN
Let's Go Plant Today	Richards	Stephen	119	ps		
Light One Candle	Yarrow	Peter	114		PR	IN
Lo Alecha	Freelander, Klepper	Daniel, Jeffrey	281		PR	IN
Lo Yisa Goy	Altman	Sharon	268	ps	PR	IN
Los Bilbilicos	Ladino Folk Song		17			IN
Mah Nishtanah	Friedman	Debbie	152	ps	PR	IN
	Haggadah Chant		156	ps	PR	IN
	Israeli Tune		154	ps	PR	IN
Mah Tovu	Folk Song		206	ps	PR	IN
Mah Yafeh Hayom	Miron	Issachar	73	ps	PR	
Maoz Tzur	Ashkenazic Melody		112		PR	IN
Mayim, Mayim	Amiran	Emanuel	174		PR	IN
Menorah	Klepper	Jeffrey	190	ps	PR	
Mezuzah	Klepper	Jeffrey	189	ps		PR
Mi Chamocha	Ashkenazic Melody		111			IN
	Freed	Isadore	215			IN
	Shirat Hayam Chant		259			IN
	Traditional Nusach		88			IN
Mi Chamocha-Pesach	Traditional		142			IN
Mi Chamocha-Shavuot	Traditional		187		PR	IN
Mi Chamocha-Sukkot	Traditional		102			IN
Mi Y'maleil	Ravino	M.	118		PR	IN
Mishpachah Song	Syme	Daniel	30	ps	PR	
Modeh Ani	Klepper, Freelander	Jeffrey, Daniel	205		PR	IN
Noah and the Ark	Funk	Joel	253	ps	PR	
Now We Say Shalom	Richards	Stephen	11	ps	PR	
Od Yishama	Carlebach	Shlomo	57			IN
On Shabbat	Paley	Cindy	67	ps	PR	
Oseh Shalom	Friedman	Debbie	218		PR	IN
	Hirsch	Nurit	216	ps	PR	IN

Title	Last Name	First Name	Page	Pre-Sch	Primary	Intermediate
Oseh Shalom	Klepper	Jeffrey	217		PR	IN
Ot Pustyi Narod Moi	Folk Song		296			IN
Oyfn Pripichok	Warshawsky	Mark	36			IN
People In My Synagogue	Moss	Jeffrey	195	ps		
Pesach Is Here Today	Reuben	Steven Carr	131	ps	PR	IN
Planting Song	Klepper	Jeffrey	120		PR	
Prayer is Reaching	Klepper	Jeffrey	203		PR	
Purim Game	Friedman	Debbie	122	ps	PR	
Purim's A Time	Auerbach	Julie Jaslow	124	ps	PR	
Rabbi	Klepper	Jeffrey	198	ps	PR	
Rise snd Shine	Folk Song		251	ps	PR	
Rojinkes Mit Mandlen	Goldfaden	Abraham	18			IN
S'vivon	Folk Song		117	ps	PR	
Say the B'rachot	Reuben	Steven Carr	201	ps	PR	
Seder Plate Song	Bar-Nissim	Barbara	134	ps	PR	
Seder Table	Friedman	Debbie	132	ps	PR	
Sh'ma	Pik	Tzivika	211	ps	PR	IN
Shabbat Shalom	Frankel	Nachum	63	ps	PR	
Shabbat, Shabbat Shalom	Auerbach	Julie Jaslow	68	ps		
Shalom Aleichem	Goldfarb	Samuel	77			IN
Shalom-Tree of Life	Silverman	Richard	230		PR	IN
Shavua Tov	Klepper	Jeffrey	74	ps	PR	
Shavuot	Reuben	Steven Carr	185	ps	PR	
Shehecheyanu	Pik	Tzivika	62	ps	PR	IN
	Traditional Nusach		61	ps	PR	IN
Shir Baboker Baboker	Artzi, and Koren	S and G	175		PR	IN
Simon Tov	Chassidic Folk Song		56	ps	PR	IN
Sing Along Song	Reuben	Steven Carr	86	ps	PR	
Sisu Et Y'rushalayim	Nof	Akiva	179		PR	IN
S'lichah, Todah, B'vakashah	Shurin	Ella	26	ps	PR	
Stir the Soup	Gewirtz	Gladys	69	ps		
Sukkot Morning	Cook	Ray	98	ps	PR	
Sukkot Song	Reuben	Steven Carr	100		PR	
Synagogue	Klepper	Jeffrey	188	ps	PR	
Tapuchim Ud'vash	Folk Song		85	ps	PR	
Ten Commandments Song	Klepper	Jeffrey	260		PR	
Thank You God	Reuben	Steven Carr	42		PR	
The Rainbow Covenant	Solomon	Robert	299		PR	IN
This Is Very Good	Klepper	Jeffrey	249	ps	PR	
To Build a Sukkah	Friedman	Debbie	99	ps	PR	
To See the World Through Jewish Eyes	Reuben	Steven Carr	44		PR	IN
Tora Li	Reuben	Steven Carr	103	ps	PR	
Torah	Klepper	Jeffrey	246		PR	
Torah Blessings	Traditional		225			IN
Torah Service: Ki Mitzion	Sulzer	Solomon	222			IN
Torah Service: Sh'ma	Sulzer, Ephros	Solomon, Gershon	223	ps	PR	IN
Tumbalalaika	Folk Song		14	ps	PR	IN
Tzenah, Tzenah	Grossman	I.	12		IN	
Ufaratzta	Chassidic		257		PR	IN
V'ahavta	Isaacson	Michael	212		PR	IN
	Torah Chant		262			IN
V'nomar L'fanav	Chassidic		242		PR	IN
V'zot Hatorah	Idelsohn	A.Z.	227			IN
We Say "Shehecheyanu"	Klepper	Jeffrey	32	ps	PR	IN
What is a Mitzvah	Bar-Nissim	Barbara	284	ps	PR	
When We March On Simchat Torah	Friedman	Debbie	104	ps	PR	
With My Family	Klepper	Jeffrey	33	ps	PR	
World of Our Fathers	Solomon	Robert	20			IN
Y'rushalayim	Folk Song		180		PR	IN
Yad B'yad	Taubman	Craig	293		PR	IN
Yism'chu Hashmayim	Chassidic		207	ps	PR	IN
Yisrael V'oraita	Folk Song		186		PR	IN
You Can Share the World	Klepper	Jeffrey	128		PR	IN
Zog Nit Keinmol	Pokras		161			IN
Zum Gali Gali	Folk Song		171	ps	PR	IN

INDEX BY COMPOSER